THE TRUTH ABOUT THE SECRET

By
STEPHANIE DiTOMMASO

Copyright © 2008 by Stephanie DiTommaso

The Truth About The Secret
by Stephanie DiTommaso

Printed in the United States of America

ISBN 978-1-60647-404-4

All rights reserved solely by the author. The author guarantees all contents are original and do not infringe upon the legal rights of any other person or work. No part of this book may be reproduced in any form without the permission of the author. The views expressed in this book are not necessarily those of the publisher.

Unless otherwise indicated, Bible quotations are taken from The Holy Bible, New International Version, Copyright © 1973, 1978, 1984 by International Bible Society, Use by permission of Zondervan Publishing House, and The New American Standard Bible, Copyright © 1960, 1962, 1963,1968, 1971, 1972, 1973, 1975, 1977, 1995 by The Lockman Foundation, and The Holy Bible in the Contemporary English Version, Copyright © 1995 by American Bible Society.

Other Bibles Used: E-Sword Version 7.8.5, (2000-2007), Rick Meyers www.e-sword.net, Good News Bible-Second Edition, (1992). American Bible

Society and King James Version of the Holy Bible (1850 revision). Strong's Exhaustive Concordance by James Strong, S.T.D., LL.D., 1890

www.xulonpress.com

TABLE OF CONTENTS

Acknowledgements vii
Foreword ix
Introduction viii
According To The Secret 19
The Father Of Lies 27
The Truth Is For You 35
The Truth Revealed 47
How To Use The Truth 67
God's Powerful Process 93
The Truth About Money 105
The Truth About Relationships 113
The Truth About Health 127
The Truth About The World 137
The Truth About You 141
The Truth About Life 153
References 161

ACKNOWLEDGEMENTS

To my devoted husband, Nicky, thank you for enduring the numerous, lonely nights as I eagerly typed away to write my very first book. Thank you for always believing in me, even when I couldn't believe in myself. You are my greatest encourager and I love you deeply.

To my children, Kayla, Taylor, and Christian, thank you for all the joy you bring to my life. Without you, I may not have wanted to know God. Each of you makes my heart smile and my lips sing.

To my step-mom, Brenda, without you I would still be broken. Thank you for helping to heal my wounded heart. You are the closest example of Christ I know. Thank you for loving me.

To my friends, thank you for always lending your ears, while caring for my children. Thank you for your friendship. Each one of you is an answered prayer from my heavenly Father.

To each of you, this book is written so that you may know the one, true God. My prayer is that you would experience the indescribable, holy presence of

His Son, Jesus. May He guide your steps straight into His loving arms.

FOREWARD

Over the centuries, there have been many innovative philosophies and ideas to help you better your life and accomplish your dreams. Many of them have proven beneficial and effective. The truth is we can certainly work hard for what we want out of life, we can dream, write down those dreams and post them on our walls for inspiration. We can strive to achieve those dreams, and many of us do. But that only lasts a lifetime. What about eternity? The reality is many people have formed their own opinions and ideas about life and life after death, but many of those concepts are false.

I write to you concerning the indisputable, authentic, existing Truth. And I invite you to follow along with me, to allow me to guide you in the Truth behind the deceptions of this world.

Discover your purpose on this earth and how to achieve the dream the Creator has for you, and find out the Truth concerning eternal life.

When I first heard about *The Secret*, I was skeptical. How could a philosophy sound so good to me without the discourse of our Creator to back it up? We all have heard ideas and theologies that make sense to us, some of which are so compelling an argument that we can't help but agree. As I read *The Secret*, I found many underlying truths - all of which I will discuss. *The Secret* is a world-renowned book and has become a household name.

My passion lies within the Truth behind *The Secret*. While this and other new age philosophies do an excellent job of explaining how to dream and even how to obtain the dreams we create, *The Secret* did fall short in several areas.

I will discuss *The Secret*'s principles and then explain what the Bible says about their philosophy. My desire is that you will not only know my Lord and Savior, but that you too will choose Him as yours. My desire is for you to know Him as I do. I will explain how you can have a relationship with your heavenly Father so that He can bless your life and all that is in it.

I will be using the New International Version (NIV) of the Bible in most texts. In addition, I will use: The New American Standard Bible, (NASB), the Good News Bible (GNB), and the Contemporary English Version (CEV). The Scriptures quoted and not biblically referenced will come from the New International Version.

Rhonda Byrne, a writer of *The Secret*, capitalized the word "You" because she wanted the reader to know she wrote the book for you. I will be capitalizing the word "Truth" because this book is written to you, but written through Jesus Christ, who is the Truth of life.

I encourage you to read through *The Truth About The Secret* with an open mind and an approachable heart. There are many truths written for you and to help you have the life God so greatly desires for you.

INTRODUCTION

This book is written to anyone, a believer or non-believer, who has been deceived by any idea or philosophy not taught through God's Word. I believe that the principles discussed in *The Secret* have some truth, but what is necessary to say is that these principles applied *through* Christ Jesus is the Truth to *The Secret*.

It is vital to share any half-truths expressed in *The Secret*. The authors have written the book in such a convincing way that anyone would be inclined to believe their logic and scientific theories. My heart aches for those who have been misled into believing those un-truths. As a Believer in Christ, it is my responsibility to the Lord to present you with the authentic Truth. I want you to understand that my words are not written in vain nor are they meant to retaliate against what the writers of *The Secret* have said. It is my prayer for the Holy Spirit to guide you in this endeavor as you search for the authentic Truth.

When I first learned of *The Secret*, I was very intrigued and honestly, I was excited that many people had changed the quality of their lives because of what *The Secret* taught them. But I had one reservation – God was not part of the equation.

If I did not know Jesus Christ as my personal savior, the lover of my soul, and the reason for my life, *The Secret* is the system in which I would put my hopes and dreams. *The Truth About the Secret* is written so that you too can make the distinction between the Truths and the lies. The Truth is we can do all things *through Christ* who empowers us (Philippians 4:13, emphasis mine). By my own power, I cannot perform miracles and manifest that which I desire. Jesus is the Way, the Truth, and the Life (John 14:6), the way to abundant living. Hence, the endorsement of Jesus Christ is what is missing from *The Secret*.

Since the beginning of time, people have created their own gods. Some of these false teachers adapted belief systems that worship the things like the sun and the moon, and the cows and statues. Today we are taught to worship ourselves because we are in control of our lives; we are the gods of the universe. The Apostle Paul warned the people about false gods. "See to it, then, that no one enslaves you by means of the worthless deceit of human wisdom, which comes from the teachings handed down by human beings and from the ruling spirits of the universe, and not from Christ." Because in Christ Jesus are all the treasures of wisdom and knowledge. (Colossians 2:8,3 GNB).

The Secret teaches, "*The Secret* is the law of attraction. The greatest teachers who have ever lived have told us that the law of attraction is the most powerful law in the Universe." The Law of Attraction states that like attracts like. Anything that can be thought of long enough eventually comes true - both the good and the bad.

For example, if you think about becoming wealthy, then you will become wealthy, whereas if you think about all the debt you have, then you will continue to be in debt. According to the writers of *The Secret*, this is true. I have grave concern for all those who believe that. I have read over the biographies of the influencers of this book and while they seem to be educated and sincere, the reality is they aren't expressing the Truth at all.

The Truth is the Lord is the one who gives the desires of your heart and makes your plans succeed (Psalms 20:4). He searches the heart and examines the mind, to reward a man according to his conduct, according to what his deeds deserve (Jeremiah 17:10). The Lord God created you (Genesis 1:1). You are not the creator of your life. You do not get to fill that "blackboard" *The Secret* talks about.

Paul, an apostle for Jesus Christ, says that every word in the Bible is God breathed (2 Timothy 3:16), that the Lord has spoken to the writers and they have written what the Lord says so that we may understand and know the one and only, true God.

Many people search for answers to life, to their purpose in this world. Others realize this endeavor and prey upon it. They write books and stories to entice people to their point of view. Even preachers and teachers of all religions and philosophies say that their way is the right way.

How do we know the Truth? Who is right? Some would say that they are all right. The problem with that is that they all contradict each other. Even the teachers can be hypocrites. As a result, we are left confused and deterred in such a way we throw our hands up and say that there is no God and no form of true religion.

There is hope. There is a way to find Truth. It is in the Bible. Search and you will find all the answers. God promises that if you seek Him with all your heart, you will find Him (Jeremiah 29:13). He says to search the scriptures to find Truth (Acts 17:11).

Don't take the words of self-proclaimed prophets. Don't heed the advice of a co-worker or a friend just because he or she says so. Look for yourself and God will reveal Himself to you.

As I write this book, I have asked the Lord to guide me, to reveal Himself to me and give me the wisdom to discern the Truth from a lie. He has done just that. Recently, a friend of mine finished reading the book, *The Traveler's Gift*. She said that while she was reading through the first couple of chapters, she thought to give it to me to read, thinking I would be able to use some of the principles in that book for this one. I read it in one sitting, front to back. The Lord showed me a bit of who He is in that book – giving, forgiving, understanding, compassionate and a God of second chances. I was truly amazed; He had answered a fraction of my prayer thus far. I couldn't wait for what was next.

The Truth About The Secret

I prayed, asked God to guide me, and He did. He hasn't stopped. Everyday, I am amazed at His faithfulness. You too can ask the Lord to guide you in Truth. When you seek the Lord, He will reveal Himself to you.

From the depths of my heart, I urge you to seek Him. I grieve for those who won't bother to open a single page. The Lord says to those who refuse Him, He will "give" them over to their own hearts' desires (Romans 1:24). Thereby allowing you to be saddened with your own beliefs.

The Secret is a composite of many writers who have placed their philosophies and experiences into one book. Most of the writers have excellent credentials and a great deal of experience in the field in which they are writing. Their messages are believable and compelling and some of them true.

Journey with me as I write the facts according to *The Bible*. Learn why we are so easily deceived and discover the marvelous Truth as we distinguish the difference between truth and deception.

> "My people are destroyed from lack of Knowledge" (Hosea 4:6).

> "There is no better book with which to defend the Bible than the Bible itself." D.L. Moody

> "Unless I am convinced by Scripture and plain reason — I do not accept the authority of popes and councils, for they contradicted each other—my conscience is captive to the

word of God. I cannot recant anything, for to go against my conscience is neither right nor safe. Here I stand; I cannot do otherwise. God help me, Amen." Martin Luther

ACCORDING TO THE SECRET

"We all work with one infinite power. We guide ourselves by exactly the same laws. The natural laws of the universe are so precise... Wherever you are...we are all working with one power. One Law. It's the law of attraction. *The Secret* is the law of attraction." This is what Bob Proctor, a philosopher, author and personal coach, teaches in the recent self-help book, *The Secret*.

The writers of *The Secret* claim that this philosophy applied to all aspects of daily living will lead you to a prosperous life and you "will begin to understand the hidden, untapped power that's within you." Rhonda Byrne, the writer of *The Secret* says, "fragments of a Great Secret have been found in the oral traditions, in literature, in religions and philosophies throughout centuries." In essence, Byrne says that applying *The Secret* will eliminate disease, overcome adversity, achieve great success and accomplish the impossible.

The writers declare that we attract everything in our lives; our thoughts are a real force that manifests itself into reality. They say that many religions and great teachers have known that the law of attraction is the most powerful in the universe and that this law has existed since the beginning of time.

John Assaraf, an entrepreneur and money making expert, says that we are like magnets. Bob Doyle, an author and law of attraction specialist says, "Like attracts like."

Proctor said, "If you see it in your mind, you're going to hold it in your hand." So, according to Bob Proctor, if we think positively, we will send positive thoughts into the Universe, thereby creating good things that will come to us.

Could the reverse be true as well? For example, as I sit here writing this book, I continue to be interrupted with phone calls, work, children, husband, friends, and bathroom breaks; the list is endless. *The Secret* claims that those thoughts magnetically will lead to continuous interruptions because the frequency my mind put out has summoned the Universe for them.

In addition, *The Secret* claims that this law of attraction works with the bad as well as the good energy flowing through your thoughts. Doyle said, "The law of attraction doesn't care whether you perceive something to be good or bad, or whether you don't want it or whether you do want it. It's responding to your thoughts.

"So if you're looking at a mountain of debt, feeling terrible about it, that's the signal you're putting out into the Universe. 'I feel really bad because of all this debt I've got.' You're just affirming it to yourself. You feel it on every level of your being. That's what you're going to get more of."

Essentially, *The Secret* says you have the power to control every situation, every circumstance in your life by simply changing the way you think.

The Secret is in essence guaranteeing success to everyone who puts it to the test. If you have been following the excitement of this book and its effects, you know there is a great mixed bag of results. As a matter of fact, many people were so encouraged by this message they leaped off the couches, applied the "law of attraction" and found themselves on the *Oprah Show*.

Amanda claims her life was changed when she chose to apply the principles of *The Secret*. She and her husband were on the verge of divorce when she saw the segment of *The Secret* on *Oprah*. She heard one of the guest speakers say that gratitude is one of the keys to leading a fulfilled life. She then realized that she had created the life she has now and is ultimately responsible. Immediately she turned her thoughts around and became grateful for her life and for her husband. She and her husband have resolved their issues and are now back into a happy marriage.

Angela was still grieving deeply for the loss of her husband after the horrific tragedy of September 11. She said she had an "awakening" after she heard the message of *The Secret*. She immediately began to journal, realizing she too had created this "path of negative energy" and she wanted to start a new path toward happiness.

Lisa was another woman who claims her life was changed. She too realized that she was in a downward spiral and found the tool to turn her life around. By applying the tools in *The Secret*, Lisa left her life of depression and created an attitude transformation. She is now a happily married newlywed, with an adorable son and a successful business she created.

There are numerous accounts of people who have benefited from this knowledge. The common factor is that they had a particular moment in which they finally woke up. The "oh yeah" factor hit and clarity for their future had suddenly been exposed to them. It was a moment of truth that reverberated from within.

Oprah said, "People are hungry for guidance and meaning in their lives and *The Secret* offers some of that."

Oprah is right; *The Secret* offers *some* of that and that is why the truth resonates and allows for some hope in the changing of many lives. There are however, some aspects of *The Secret* that need to be explored – both truths and lies.

Maureen Doyle, a believer in Christ, bravely stood up and asked the question on my mind and many others' as well. "We teach our children to put their faith in God, and it seems *The Secret* tells you to put your faith in yourself. So I was wondering, is God anywhere in this?"

Michael Beckwith, a Visionary and Founder of Agape International Spiritual Center, replied.

"Absolutely. What *The Secret* is telling you is that the laws of the Universe to a limited degree describe the nature of how God works. God is the same yesterday, today, and forever – changeless. And so these laws are a limited description of the presence of God. Now when you study the prophet, Jesus, the Christ, he used the language, 'pray believing that ye have that ye may receive.' That is *The Secret* in a nutshell. Pray believing and feeling and sensing that you already have it and then you are available to receive it. *The Secret* doesn't contradict any religion, it actually goes underneath the culture and explains to you the sacred laws these wonderful teachers have brought to us."

Ms. Doyle asked another. "I did see that Neale Donald Walsch in his part of *The Secret*, said, 'You would not stand in judgment to no one ever, now or ever.' What I got out of it was…you wouldn't have to answer to anyone."

Beckwith replied, "No, the thoughts that you do, the energy that you place out, you experience that. It's not that you go to hell, but the choices you make if they are limiting, if you feel that limitation, you put yourself in prison. If you make choices that are loving, compassionate, giving, forgiving expression. The way Jesus described it was, 'The kingdom of heaven is at hand now.' Heaven means the realm of ever expanding good. So the realm of ever expanding good is always at hand now based on the choices that you are making. And everyone is accountable for the things they do and don't do."

After other conversation, Ms. Doyle answered Oprah, "Yes, I believe there is a heaven and hell."

James Arthur Ray said, "Consider this. Jesus Christ said the kingdom of heaven in within. He didn't say it was somewhere; it's within. So isn't it possible to consider the kingdom of hell is within as well and it's your choice as to what you are going to create."

Beckwith agreed with Mr. Ray, saying, "That's what I was going to say. The kingdom of heaven is actually within us. That what comes out of your mouth, what you think about, how you express that, you are either participating in the realm of ever expanding good or you are cutting yourself off from the realm of ever expanding good."

Dr. Joe Vital, a metaphysical practitioner, certified hypnotherapist, ordained minister, and Chi Kung healer believes, "Everything that surrounds you right now in your life, including the things you're complaining about, you've attracted... This is one of the hardest concepts to get, but once you've accepted it, it's life transforming."

Lisa Nichols, an advocate of personal empowerment, says that your feelings make you feel bad or they make you feel good. According to Lisa, you can intentionally choose to feel good so that you can bring good back from the universe.

Michael Bernard Beckwith summed it up this way. "You can begin right now to feel healthy. You can begin to feel prosperous. You can begin to feel the love that's surrounding you, even if it's not there. And what will happen is the universe will correspond

The Truth About The Secret

to the nature of your song. The universe will correspond to the nature of that inner feeling and manifest, because that's the way you feel."

Marci Shimoff said, "Our emotions let us know what we are thinking. Once you begin to understand and truly master your thoughts and feelings, that's when you see how you create your own reality... that's where all your power is."

Rhonda Byrne held that love is the greatest emotion, the greatest power in the Universe. She referenced the great thinkers of the past who "referred to the law of attraction as the law of love. So if your predominant state is love, the law of attraction or the law of love responds with the mightiest force because you are on the highest frequency possible. The greater the love you feel and emit, the greater the power you are harnessing."

Beckwith believes that gratitude is an important factor in changing your life. "Nothing new can come into your life without gratitude. The moment you begin to focus on gratitude, you create the condition for yourself for more things to come into your life" (*Oprah Show*).

In summation, according to *The Secret*, the secret is the law of attraction.

This law is, to a limited degree, descriptive of how God works and it lies beneath the cultures and religion the great teachers have taught us. Since the "kingdom of heaven is within," we choose what we create. Thus having power over our thoughts and emotions, we control the Universe.

When we become filled with love and gratitude, we send those emotions through a field of energy that brings back love and gratitude. The writers of *The Secret* explain how to use the law of attraction and gain control of your mind to see your dreams come to fruition in every aspect of your life.

In the subsequent chapters, I will discuss their perspectives in conjunction with the truths of the Bible.

THE FATHER OF LIES

Look around. This world becomes increasingly self-indulgent. We work so hard to possess so many materialistic things. Yet, we are never happy with what we have: our looks, our homes, our cars, our money, our friends or even our spouses. We are always looking for a way to have more or make things "better" than they are. Many are seeking affluence, prominence, power, and self-gratification to which is all meaninglessness. Does that really lead to a peaceful, joyful life that we all aspire to have?

Make-believe with me for a moment… Imagine everyone in this world is equal in his or her possessions. We all have the same ranch style home with the same four-door vehicle and no job for which we need money. We don't have any need for money because we all have the necessary items we need for daily living. The only differences in us are our personalities and our physical characteristics.

We each have our own gifts and talent for which we flourish. There is no need to be better than we are because we all excel in our respective talents. All that is left is for us to share personal gifts with each other. What would you do? How would you share yourself? How would you express who you are and what would be the point of it? Maybe the purpose would be peace and joy, contentment and gratification?

This, I believe, is our mission in life, for each and every person. What a joy it would bring to know you have made a difference in the life of another simply by being who you are without any pretenses or worries. The greatest concern in your life may just be whether or not you gave a bit of yourself to someone else.

Now, take a moment to come back to the real world, a world that is consumed with exceedingly emotional people. People who try to fulfill their emptiness with any way they know how. For some of us it is food, or alcohol, or physical pleasures and insatiability. It is so difficult for us to look within ourselves to confront who we really are.

Those indulgences are all worldly things; things of the "universe" created to distract us from the Truth of God. The Truth is that our gluttony and self-indulgence stem from pride. That is the same pride that sent the father of lies to deceive us.

There is a very real power in this universe. Energy so powerful that it can allow your visions and dreams to come true. This force in the world can cheer you on in your idea of success. You think it, you say it, you believe it and yes this spirit can and *often* times will bring your dream to reality. This energy is not the law of attraction; this spirit is a created super being. We know him as Satan.

The Scriptures say that Satan is a fallen angel. He was one of the first to be created by God. God said that he was the "model of perfection, full of wisdom and perfect in beauty." God ordained him as the guardian angel and made him blameless in all his ways. However, the Lord created all of the angels to have free will; they were fully able to reject the will of God. Satan's heart became proud on account of his beauty and he declared himself to be like the "Most High" God.

Satan thought he was all-powerful and too beautiful for God and his angels in heaven. He felt he was so influential that he could overthrow God's kingdom. Satan now prowls around on earth with his crew of angels who fell with him searching for those he can manipulate into sin. (Isaiah 14:12-15, Ezekiel 28:11-18).

Satan is now, and has been, at war with God for God's people (Christians). Satan wants to place doubt in our faith and in our minds that God is present. But, he is not allowed to harm or deceive those who love God, without God's permission (Job 1:12).

The Lord wants to test us so that He can put us into a position to serve Him, but Satan comes at us to do his evil bidding. He tries to turn God's plan upside down.

Matthew 4:1-11 gives a perfect example of Satan's deceit. The Spirit of God (Holy Spirit) led Jesus into the desert where he fasted for forty days and nights. Satan came to tempt Jesus by creating the doubt of what God really says, and thereby tried to lead Jesus to disobey God. Three times the devil questioned Jesus' authority, but on the third, the devil took Jesus on top of a high mountain and showed Him all the magnificent kingdoms of the world. He told Jesus that he would give Him all of it, the riches, the land, and the authority over the earth, if He would bow down and worship him (Satan).

Jesus replied, "Away from me Satan! For it is written: 'Worship the Lord your God, and serve him only.'" The devil then left Jesus and the angels of heaven came to comfort Him (thereby showing God's love and mercy).

We are the Lord's beloved and what more to hurt God than to destroy His children? As the illustration demonstrates, Satan doesn't give up when a person accepts Jesus Christ as his personal savior; he has a strategy for believers, which is very subtle, and devious.

Jesus told his disciples "that Satan was a murderer from the beginning, not holding to the Truth, for there is no Truth in him. When he lies, he speaks his native language, for he is a liar and the father of lies" (John 8:44). He prances around like a roaring lion looking for someone to devour (1 Peter 5:8). He is cunning, intelligent and never looks out for our well-being.

Satan tries to prevent the believer from knowing God's Word. He encourages Christians to ignore the Scriptures and accept false teaching so that they will revert to their previous way of life.

1Timothy 4:1 says, "...Some will abandon the faith and follow deceiving spirits and things taught by demons."

The Apostle Paul also explains in 2 Corinthians 2:11 that "Satan may outwit us for we are unaware of his schemes."

This is why I write to you the Truth about *The Secret*, so that you will be conscious of the deceit and aware of the schemes taught by men.

Jesus called Satan the prince of this world (John 12:31).

The word "world" in the Greek form means "kosmos" meaning the orderly arrangement of things, which includes the inhabitants of the earth (*Strong's Concordance*).Therefore, Satan has dominion and authority over this world, including people and all of its inhabitants. Not only is Satan here to deceive and distract Christians, but he also does his best to destroy the non-believer's ability to triumph over him. The non-believer's way of defeating the devil is to see him, as he really is – a liar and a deceiver. The devil is the one who promotes self-centeredness, greed, insatiability, and chaos in this world.

Luke 8:12 says, "the devil comes and takes away the word from their hearts, so that they may not believe and be saved." But when anyone believes in his heart that God raised Christ from the dead and confesses with your mouth that Jesus Christ is Lord, you shall be saved (Romans 10:9). However, if you believe and do not mix that belief with faith, the devil will do his best to distract you from your belief. You must act out that belief through your exemplified faith.

Place your faith in Christ, don't let Satan rule over your hearts.

Jesus warns us to "Watch out! Be on your guard against all kinds of greed; a man's life does not consist in the abundance of his possessions" (Luke 12:15).

The Apostle Paul encourages us to rejoice in the Lord always (not in the stuff that we have) and then the peace of God will guard your heart and mind in Christ Jesus (Philippians 4:4,7).

Satan can't read your mind, he is not omniscient; he doesn't know everything. The only way Satan can know how to tempt you personally is by what you say and or do. Keep in mind, there are many angels of Satan to watch your actions in order to tempt you to do wrong. After all, they have had thousands of years of practice to examine human behavior. This is why it is so important for you to control your thoughts.

If you do not guard your heart and mind with what the Lord says, you can allow your thoughts to be controlled by the devil. I am not saying that what you do is either from Satan or God. However, if you are not a believer in Christ, Satan already has a hold on you. The Apostle Paul tells us in Ephesians 2:2 that people who are disobedient, automatically allow Satan, the ruler of the kingdom of the air, the spirit to work in them.

Your thoughts can lead you to what you say. *The Secret* is right about that. The problem is that the devil, the prince of the people on earth, knows it too. Jesus tells us that "The prince of this world is coming…but the world must *learn* that I love the Father and that I do exactly what my Father has commanded me" (John 14:30-31, emphasis mine). That is why it is vital to control your thoughts. I will discuss how to do this in the subsequent chapters.

It is the desire of Satan to alter our behavior to accomplish his evil schemes. Satan will put obstacles in your path to lead you to desire them.

The Secret focuses our ability to control our wealth, relationships, and life with our thoughts. Satan uses that to his advantage. He knows we all want more of anything or everything – it's the nature of our being. We are human.

The Secret stems from Satan doing what he does best. Rousing you into thinking that you are capable of having all the earthly possessions you want. Presenting you as the god of your life will only send you down into the depths of the pit with him. So when *The Secret* says that you are god, you are the creator, can you not see that their message is setting you up to be like the "Most High" God?

Because the devil imitates God and because he wants to deceive the believers of Christ, he imitates God by showing us what we can have and by doing what God would do. Satan takes us captive to do his will (2 Timothy 2:26).

We have learned that it has been Satan's goal from the beginning to defeat God. Therefore, it is our primary responsibility to open our hearts and minds and fill it with the knowledge and Truth of God. And then listen to Him and act out of obedience.

You can defeat the father of lies, the prince of this world. You can set your mind on things above, not on earthly things (Colossians 3:2).

Remember our make-believe moment? Start a new life for you. Seek out whose you are and ask the Lord for guidance and direction in your life. Start by giving more of yourself and receiving fewer indulgences. God is waiting for you.

The worldly things will come and go, but the Truth of Jesus Christ will remain. Jesus said that His kingdom is not of this world (Satan's rule), and He has asked our Lord to teach us the Truth of who He is through a relationship with Christ.

> "False prophets will appear and perform great signs and miracles to deceive even the elect…" (Jesus Christ, Matthew 24:24).

> "The devil can counterfeit all the saving operations and graces of the Spirit of God." Jonathan Edwards

> "The enemy will not see you vanish into God's company without an effort to reclaim you." C.S. Lewis

> "The devil can cite Scripture for his purpose." William Shakespeare

> You must examine the scriptures for yourself to determine what is true (Acts 17:11).

THE TRUTH IS FOR YOU

We all have a strong desire to be like God. After all, God is perfect, powerful, and infinite. Since the beginning of time, man has struggled to be like God. Eve ate from the forbidden fruit because the serpent told her she would be just like God. Satan was thrown from heaven because he placed himself, "like the Most High God."

Even today, books like *The Secret* are telling you that you are a god. You are the creator of your life. You are energy, God is energy, and therefore you are a god. Why wouldn't you want to believe that? If you hold the power from within to control your future, your universe and your creation, why then can't you control your children?

Satan misled Eve when he told her that her eyes would be opened and she would be like God, knowing good and evil. He created a seed of doubt when he asked, "did God really say?" (Genesis 3:1). But once she ate from the forbidden fruit, immediately her eyes were opened to their nakedness and

The Truth About The Secret

she felt shame, she did know the difference between good and evil, but never would she be like God.

Satan is the ultimate deceiver. *The Secret* is a perfect example of deceit – crafty and cunning. We may be energy, but we are not God, nor are we a god.

John Assaraf said, "Everything is made up of the exact same thing, whether it's your hand, the ocean, or a star." Dr. Ben Johnson agrees, "Everything is energy."

James Ray takes this theory a step further to help us understand. He explains, "Even under a microscope you're an energy field. You go to a quantum physicist and you say, 'what creates the world?' And he or she will say, 'Energy.' Well, describe energy. 'OK, it can never be created or destroyed, it always was, always has been, everything that ever existed always exists, it's moving into form, through form and out of form.'

"You go to a theologian and ask the question, 'What created the Universe?' And he or she will say, 'God.' OK, describe God. 'Always was and always has been, never can be created or destroyed, all that ever was, always will be, always moving into form, through form and out of form.' You see it's the same description, just different terminology."

That is their theory, of course. But, let me explain in further detail. The teachers of *The Secret* tried to explain that our spirit moves in and out of forms, that we just physically die while our spirit moves on into another form of life.

Yes, humans are finite beings; our body was made from the dust and we will return to the dust. However, our spirit will be held for judgment and live for an eternity with our heavenly Father or in the depths of the fiery abyss with Satan. Scripture tells us that man is destined to die once and then, after that, to face judgment (Hebrews 9:27). That means when we die on earth, immediately our spirit goes before the Lord.

Rhonda Byrne explains that we will always be and asks us if we could imagine not being. What I can't imagine is my spirit spending eternal life suffering, tormenting and burning in the eternal flames of hell. However, what I can imagine is kneeling in the presence of my precious Savior giving Him praises for all He has done. God breathed our spirit into us. When He made Adam, the first man, from the dust of the earth, God breathed life into him and he became a living being (Genesis 2:7).

The Lord created us in His image (Genesis 1:26), to be holy, righteous, worthy of honor and someday we will be the way He intended us to be. When we strive to have the character of God, our spirit will exude His character. So when God says we are created to be like Him, what we will become is solely based on what we feed our spirit here on earth. Paul tells us in 1 John 3:2, "My dear friends, we are now God's children, but it is not clear what we shall become. But we know that when Christ appears, we shall be like him, because we shall see him as he really is" (GNB).

We know from the example of the resurrected Jesus that our spiritual bodies will be similar to our physical bodies. They will not be the same body, but a glorified one however (1 Corinthians 15:40); free to go in and out of locked doors and appear wherever we want (John 20:19). We will be able to eat and drink, but most importantly, we will be free of sin, made after the holiness of Christ (1 John 3:2).

Lisa Nichols said that our body is our physical being and it holds our spirit. Yes, our bodies are filled with a spirit, but only when you acknowledge and accept that Jesus Christ came to save us from eternal death does your spirit become eternal life.

Jesus said, "Flesh gives birth to the flesh, but the Spirit gives birth to the Spirit. You must be born again [in the Spirit] to see the kingdom of God" (John 3:6,7,3). Otherwise the spirit that resides in you will lead to eternal death.

If we are living a life of sin, if we have an unforgiving spirit, if we are faithless and living without obedience to God, we are living according to our flesh. That kind of living only multiplies sinful living; we do reap what we sow. Conversely, if we are living a life through the Spirit of God, we will have a forgiving heart, we will be full of faith in Christ and therefore multiply a life of peace.

Jude, Jesus' half brother encourages us to "keep yourselves in God's love as you wait for the mercy of our Lord Jesus Christ to bring you to eternal life"(Jude: 21). Jesus Christ will bring you to salvation and eternal life; we have not already received it.

Unless we acknowledge Him as our Savior, we will not have eternal life.

Nichols continues to say that we "are God manifested in human form, made to perfection." Michael Bernard Beckwith refers to Scripture to back up her claim. He said, "Scripturally we could say that we are the image and the likeness of God. We could say we are another way that the Universe is becoming conscious of itself. We could say that we are the infinite field of unfolding possibility. All of that would be true."

Nichols tried to prove this theory by saying that if we are energy and God is energy, we are God. The truth is we are made in the image of Him, in his likeness; we are not God. If we say that, we are God or a god, we are setting ourselves up for condemnation.

The Lord says, "I am the LORD your God...You shall have no other gods before me. You shall not make for yourself an idol in the form of heaven above or on the earth beneath or in the waters below... for I am the LORD your God" (Exodus 20:2-5). In Psalm 82:6, The Lord said, "You are 'gods'; you are all sons of the Most High. But you will die like mere men, you will fall like every other ruler."

The God in heaven is our Lord. He reigns over us. We are not God. You cannot just wish something into existence. You can't tell the "universe" something and demand it to come true – unless what you receive is not from God.

In your life on earth, you have many choices. God has provided a way for you to live your life and have it abundantly. You can choose eternal life, or you can choose eternal death. In the big picture, those are your only choices.

Nichols wrote, "You are the designer of your destiny. You are the author. You write the story. The pen is in your hand, and the outcome is whatever you choose." However, Psalm 139:16 says, "...All the days ordained for me were written in your book before one of them came to be."

God also helps you to make the right choices. Proverbs 16:1,9 states, "We may make our own plans, but God has the last word, God directs your actions" (GNB). Therefore, God is the Author of our destiny.

Michael Bernard Beckwith said, "And you can break yourself free from your hereditary patterns, cultural codes, social beliefs, and prove once and for all that the power within you is greater than the power within the world." You can break free from the chains of bondage through Jesus Christ in you; it is He who is that power. Otherwise the power within is you at your own will and that will prove to fail every time.

Jesus gave hope to His believers, "In this world, you will have trouble, but take heart, I have overcome the world" (John 16:33). "Greater is He who is in you, than he who is in the world" (1 John 4:4). You have the power through Christ.

This is the entire premise of my book. If you take nothing away from this book, please remember it is not by your own power to achieve greatness, but through Christ's.

God breathed life into you. He placed His hopes and desires in you. Satan came to destroy you, but Christ came to save you. Won't you put your heart in God's hand? He knows you better than you know yourself, for He created you. When you seek the Truth, God promises He will reveal the Truth to you. You will have eternal life and your earthly life will be abundant.

This is what my step-mom had to say when she decided to ask God what His will was for her, when she completely put her trust in God.

"I found myself single again and decided I wanted God to hand pick a husband for me. So over that time I occasionally would pray and ask God if the man I was dating was 'the one' He had planned for me. I had met Steve through a friend and we really hit it off. Our first date was on my birthday and he brought me some flowers. He had the same Christian values as I did and was active in his local church. So we dated for about three months and then Steve broke up with me. I was quite disappointed. He said that he wasn't ready to be serious and just wanted to be my friend. Deep down in my heart I knew that he wasn't God's man for me and that was okay because 'the one' was out there somewhere.

"Nine months went by without a word from Steve and then he called and wanted to take me out on my birthday. Well hope was rekindled. Maybe he now was ready to be serious. So I prayed for clarity. 'God, is this the right one or are we to just be friends? Lord, if he isn't the one then he won't bring me flowers.' Again, my biggest fear was to marry the wrong man.

The one thing I needed from God was a very LOUD yes or no. Well, Steve showed up for our date with guess what! Not flowers, but a plant. To this day Steve probably wonders why he chose a plant over flowers and why I was so pleased to receive this unusual gift. I was somewhat disappointed but also relieved that I would not marry the wrong man. God had a plan for me, wow! And I was determined to wait on God! It was five years later when I met 'the one' and every day that I look at the bowl that plant was in, and I thank God for his 'no'. Phillip and I have been married twelve years now. He is not perfect, but he's perfect for me. God's 'no' is just as important as His sweet, 'yes.'"

My step-mom is the happiest person I know. Of course she would like certain things in her life to be different, but she knows that God is in control. She simply places her faith in Christ and gives Him praises for all that she has. Her life is simple, peaceful, joyful and abundant. God has given her those blessings as a result of her obedience to Him.

I pray that kind of abundance for your life too. I encourage you to read and study John 3 in the Bible. It explains who Jesus is and why he came. It will help you understand who you are and why you are here and life for eternity.

THE ANCIENT BABYLONIANS

Upon reading *The Secret*, one of the first things that caught my attention was the reference to the ancient Babylonians. Bob Proctor said, "Wise people have always known this. You can go right back to the ancient Babylonians. They've always known this. It's a small select group of people."

The inference to the "wise" Babylonians is completely absurd. Let me explain. Yes, they did have vast prosperity and great scholars and the Bible have documented this. In fact, they are known for creating the Hanging Gardens of Babylon, one of the Seven Wonders of the Ancient World.

My concern for you is that you don't focus on prosperity like that of the Babylonians. Their faith was in themselves and in their idols. They were prideful and lacked the knowledge of God in Heaven.

The Secret tells you that "you are the master of your life and the Universe is answering your every command." That is wrong, not true, an utter lie and if you believe that, then it is imperative for your life that you continue to read further with me. What you read here may in fact save your life, if you let it.

The people of Babylon have always taken on this philosophy: "I will ascend above the tops of the clouds: I will make myself like the Most High (God)" (Isaiah 14:14).

The earliest account of Babylon in the Bible is in Genesis 11. The Bible says the people moved eastward to Babylon and decided to "make a name for themselves." They attempted to build a tower that would reach to the heavens. When the LORD went into the city and saw the tower, He confused their language and scattered everyone throughout the earth. The remaining people in Babylon put a halt to the building of the city. That tower was henceforth called, "The Tower of Babel."

Throughout the Bible, with talks of Babylon, the Lord shows his distaste for the people who created riches and prosperity out of pride and selfishness.

Let's look at King Nebuchadnezzar for an example. Daniel writes, "While he was walking on the roof of the royal palace of Babylon, he said, 'is not this the great Babylon *I* have built as the royal residence, by *my* might and power and for the glory of *my* majesty?' (emphasis mine)

"The words were still on his lips when a voice came from heaven, 'this is what is decreed for you, King Nebuchadnezzar: Your royal authority has been taken from you. You will be driven away from people and will live with the wild animals: you will eat grass like cattle. Seven times (which means seven years) will pass by for you until you acknowledge that the Most High is sovereign over the kingdoms of men and gives them to anyone he wishes" (Daniel 4:29-32). And that is what happened.

Years later, King Belshazzar, the grandson of King Nebuchadnezzar, had a banquet for his kingdom. At the same time, the Medes and Persians were about to invade Babylon. Because of his pride and arrogance, the king thought his land was untouchable. He was even warned by God to learn from the example of King Nebuchadnezzar.

But the King continued in his rebellion. King Belshazzar went to the extreme of drinking from the sacred goblets from the temple and worshiping other gods (gold, silver, stone, and iron and wood).

He didn't honor the God in heaven nor did he revere Him. As a result, the Lord took King Belshazzar's life and Babylon was conquered by Persia. The year was 539 B.C.

The people of Babylon were not "wise" after all.

The kings believed that they ruled the world, that they were indestructible. They told the "Universe" that they were the rulers and the almighty; they believed they were all powerful, but in the end, God showed them who was in control to the extent of death and destruction for all those who believed in themselves.

THE TRUTH REVEALED

We believe what we do as a result of our past experiences in life. For many, if their childhood was insecure at best, they may have grown up with a skeptical outlook of their environment and the people around them. Whereas if one came from a solid foundation of love and respect in the home, it is more likely for that person to have faith in others, for what is seen and unseen.

The reality is that love is the foundation for a lasting relationship. If we don't have love, if we haven't been loved, we have nothing in which to believe. For why would we? What difference in the world would it make if we believed in something we couldn't love?

My observation of society is that many of us are so consumed with ourselves that we haven't much time to really seek out Truth. If we can have philosophers and inspirational teachers tell us how to achieve the abundant life, then well, we strongly desire to grab a hold of it because it is what we want to hear. Frankly, it makes us feel good. And well, "If it feels good, do it."

So the writers of *The Secret* tell you that if you envision good health, focus on good health, say and do things that will bring you good health, and believe you will have good health, then, voila! You have good health. If you vision "the perfect mate," focus on that idea; believe that you will receive him or her, say you already have him or her, (and still go to bed alone) poof! The perfect mate appears. And what about money? We all want more of that. Again, vision more money, focus on more money, say you have more money, (while the debt collectors are calling) and bam, there's more money in your lap. Seems a bit far fetched to me, but so then do other beliefs and philosophies.

But the power of faith, the power of believing in something is so strong, anything can and virtually will happen as a result. The missing factor in the law of attraction is action. Nothing will appear from thin air because you have willed it to do so. *The Secret* says you are attracting everything that comes into your life with your thoughts.

You want to believe in something, we all do. But which idea or philosophy will hurt us less? Will we have to devote our lives to some new age plan that will make your life better and then realize that it wasn't Truth at all?

THE TRINITY

The most important Truth to establish is that Jesus is not a prophet like Michael Bernard Beckwith, the spiritual founder of the Agape International Spiritual Center explained.

Jesus is the incarnate Son of God.

Genesis 1:1 says, "In the beginning, God created..." Genesis 1:26 says, "Let us make man in our image..." The words "God" and "us" are translated from the Hebrew word Elohim, which is the plural form of God.

In Hebrew grammar, you have three forms: singular, dual, and plural. Dual is for two only. The dual form is used for things that come in pairs like eyes, ears, and hands. The word "Elohim" and the pronoun "us" are plural forms - definitely more than two - thereby referring to three or more (Father, Son, Holy Spirit). They are established as the one God, the Trinity – God the Father, God the Son, and God the Holy Spirit.

We learn from Revelation 4:11, that God the Father is the definitive source for creating the Universe and commencing all things.

John, a disciple of Christ, tells us that we learn that God the Father has placed His seal of approval on Jesus Christ to give eternal life to those who believe He is God's Son, who was sent from heaven to save us from our sins (John 6:27). When Jesus spoke to His disciples, he explained that He is accomplishing the work of His Father who sent Him (John 4:34). God the Father ordained His Son to be the propitiator of our sins. He then gave us the powerful Holy Spirit to guide us in Truth.

Jesus is the incarnate Son of God.

John 1:1-2, "In the beginning was the Word and the Word was with God, and the Word was God. He was with God from the beginning." John told us that we know that the Son of God has come and has given us understanding, so that we may know the true God (1 John 5:20).

When we live in union with Jesus Christ – we also live in union with God. This belief is what will bring eternal life. Jesus is the Christ, the Savior of the world (John 4:42). Jesus said He Himself is the anticipated Messiah, the Christ that was promised to not only the Jewish nation, but also the Gentiles (John 4:26).

Jesus said, "The Helper will come – the Spirit, who reveals the truth about God and who comes from the Father. I will send him to you from the Father, and he will speak about me" (John 15:26 GNB).

Jesus told his disciples that the Counselor [Holy Spirit] would come to convict the world of the guilt of their sin, which is their unbelief in who Jesus is. He said that the prince of this world now stands destined for death as a result of the Holy Spirit. Jesus told them that all that belongs to the Father is His and the Spirit will take from Him what is His and make it known to you.

In short, the Holy Spirit is a gift from God for those that believe Jesus Christ is the Son of God. God is our creator; Jesus is God's Son who was sent to the earth to show us how to live a godly life and

HEAVEN AND HELL

Neal Donald Walsh said, "You would not stand in judgment to no one ever, now or ever."

The Truth is there is only one lawgiver and Judge (James 4:12). God is the righteous judge of the people of the earth (Psalm 58:11). He will judge the thoughts and attitudes (Hebrews 4:12); He judges the sins of man and their secrets (Romans 2:16). Paul tells us that God will judge the living and the dead (2 Timothy 4:1).

We see this come to fruition in Revelation 20:13, "The sea gave up the dead that were in it, and death and Hades gave up the dead that were in them, and each person was judged according to what he had done."

Michael Bernard Beckwith, a man who leads other people to the know the Truth of God, misrepresented God when he said, "It's not that you go to hell…"

But, Hades *is* hell. The Bible teaches that our spirits do go to heaven or hell.

The Bible gives a few descriptions of a physical hell. For when the non-believer dies, that spirit will see the Lord in Heaven and will be sent to hell, which is described as a dark, fiery place where people will suffer torment and anguish for all eternity. Revelation 20 explains that in the end times, a fire will come down from heaven and consume Satan and

The Truth About The Secret

his accomplices. They will be thrown into a lake of burning sulfur and will be tormented day and night forever and ever.

In response to Mr. Beckwith, yes, Jesus did say, "Repent, for the kingdom of heaven is at hand", but He was telling us that our salvation is dependant on our repentance.

Beckwith and James Arthur Ray, a philosopher, lecturer, author, and creator of prosperity and human potential programs, were teaching that heaven is actually within us, and that what we say and the way we express ourselves will create heaven or hell for us.

The Truth is if you are a true believer in Christ, you are saved from condemnation and judgment. On the other hand, if you do not accept Jesus Christ as the one who knows you better than you know yourself, the one who wants more for you than you could ever hope or imagine, as your Lord and Savior, then you will face the judgment of God.

Paul explains in Romans 8:1, "There is no condemnation for those who are in union with Christ" (GNB). When people live according to their human nature their lives will result in death. People will in fact become enemies of God because they cannot obey His laws. In contrast, when people live according to what the Holy Spirit tells them, the result will be life and peace (Romans 2:8-9,12, GNB).

In the beginning, God gave Moses the Law for which we should live (The Ten Commandments). Because Eve took the forbidden fruit and disobeyed God, the sin was passed down through the bloodlines. We are all born with the curse of sin; it is a fact. Therefore, it is impossible to live by the Laws that the Lord gave Moses. We will all sin in one way or another and thus we become unacceptable to God.

Romans 3:23, "For all have sinned and fall short of the glory of God." The penalty for sin is death (Romans 6:23).

What we couldn't do in our human nature, God did. He sent His Son, Jesus in human form, just like us in our human nature, to do away with sin. God did this so that the righteous demands of God's Law would be fully satisfied in us who live according to the Spirit, and not according to human nature (Romans 8:2-3). Simply stated, when we put our faith in Jesus and what He came to the earth to do, we are covered in grace by God and therefore no longer subject to God's judgment.

That is the Truth, if we are in union with Christ, we will not be judged like those who are not unified with Him. If you do not love God and accept His commands, you will be "cutting yourself off from the realm of ever expanding good."

Please understand my heart with all that I say to you. The advantages to a Christian life are peace, joy, patience, gentleness, self-control, love, kindness, faithfulness, and freedom from guilt. You don't have to live up to anyone's expectations, you don't have to prove yourself to anyone and you don't have to condemn yourself for anything in your past. Christ gave us that gift when he died on the cross.

There is a real heaven and hell. The "new heaven and new earth" are described in Revelation 21. John, the disciple of Jesus was brought to this place by an angel of the Lord to reveal the truths of the end times. John wrote about these events to encourage the faithful in Christ to resist the demands of this world...

In the new heaven, the Believers in Christ will live there in physical, glorified bodies (1 Corinthians 15:35-58). Heaven is a physical place with twelve gates, three at each direction, (north, south, east, and west) with one angel at each gate. Scripture tells us that the city is laid out like a square with walls made of jasper and the city was pure gold. The foundation was made up of twelve precious stones, the gates were of twelve pearls and the street of the city was pure gold, like a translucent glass. Heaven will not need a sun or a moon because the glory of God will shine on it, giving light. There will not be any night, nor any wrongdoing and the gates will never close.

1 John 3:2, John tells us that we will be like Christ, in thought, heart and attitude. There will be no worries because the old order of things will have passed away (Revelation 21:4).

THE MORE THINGS CHANGE, THE MORE THEY STAY THE SAME

The Bible says King Solomon is the wisest and richest man who ever lived. He is quoted, "What has been will be again, what has been done will be done again; there is nothing new under the sun" (Ecclesiastes 3:15).

Solomon also professed that everything under the sun (apart from God) is meaningless. The only thing that matters is that we "fear God and keep his commandments, for this is the whole duty of man" (Ecclesiastes12: 8,13). Serving God is what matters, nothing else.

Can we find any new philosophy that will bring us happiness? No, God provides that (1Chronicles 29:14a). King Solomon just told us that there isn't any new infinite wisdom or new age theology that will give you a perfect life. There is no perfect life; we are all flawed.

Society tends to view "perfect" as something we wish to be. We see celebrities on the television and wish we could be like them. We endlessly judge our peers based on the clothes they wear, the cars they drive and the homes in which they live. And when we are finished critiquing them, we sulk over our own imperfections and wonder why we can't be as perfect as them. When are we going to stop looking at each other to fulfill what is empty inside of us?

In Christ, we don't have to worry about any of that anymore. We are called "Children of God" (Romans 8:16). That means that in Him we are new living beings (2 Corinthians 5:17) and all of our needs are met (Philippians 4:19). We are made perfect and heirs of God (Romans 8:17) and we are blessed with all spiritual blessings (Ephesians 1:3).

You see it is unnecessary, yet so very natural for us to judge who we are based on what others think or posses. But remember, Christ died for you, while you were still a sinner, while you were still trying to measure up to the demands of others. You don't have to do that because in Christ, you are a partaker of His divine nature (2 Peter 1:4).

HOPE & FAITH

The only answer to this bitter cycle is to call upon Christ Jesus.

Scripture says we are only made perfect through Christ's sacrifice, which was His death on the cross (Hebrews 10:14). The Lord's definition of perfect is not the same as ours. He simply wants to love us – to be our Comforter, our Provider, and our Father.

"To be made perfect," means to be cleansed of your wrongdoings, your sin. God knows that you are going to make mistakes; you are human. He just wants to be a part of what you do, day in and day out. However, He can only have a relationship with you if you have asked for forgiveness of your sins.

For example, you as a parent desire nothing more than for your child to love you and to make good decisions. But children are incapable of making right choices in every situation. You then expect your children to come to you for help and guidance. If your child isn't acknowledging your existence, how then will you be able to help?

When I was a young girl, I was told that Jesus was God's Son. He died on the cross for our sins and if I believed in Him and asked him to come into my heart, I would go to heaven. So, I believed it. After all, who wouldn't want to go to Heaven? It certainly beats Hell, the alternative I was given. As I grew up,

I continued with my faith in Jesus. It wasn't until my latter twenties that I understood exactly what all that meant - who Jesus really is.

Jesus told us that belief in Him is the only way to heaven and whoever hears the good news of Him and believes by faith will not be condemned by God, but will have eternal life in heaven. All we have to do is confess any wrongdoing and God is faithful to forgive us and He will make us righteous men and women.

God knows we can't be perfect people – Adam and Eve proved that. There was perfection all around them and in the moment they were tempted, they failed to do what God had instructed them. They gave into the temptation, which brought about sin in the world. That's why He had to send his Son, Jesus.

Jesus Christ came to this earth to be the sin that was in all of us so that we could glorify God (2 Corinthians 5:21). Satan knew he could have a hold on us otherwise. Without Christ, when we make a mistake, Satan would have a hold on us – we would have to spend eternity in hell. But, Jesus Christ put an end to the laws of the past when he died on the cross, so that by faith we can worship God and He would be able to have a relationship with us (Romans 10:4).

In order to understand that concept, I think it is important to understand who God is. First, God is love (1 John 4:16). He is incapable of anything less than love. When God created the Universe, He knew what would become of Adam and Eve. The moment He discussed their sin with them, He made them atone for their iniquity. He needed a way to connect with their hearts, to be able to see them through their sin.

The same concept can be applied when we discipline our children. I remember one morning I walked home from a sleepover. I was about eight years old. Excitedly, I swung open the door and ran to show my step-mom a shiny Susan B. Anthony coin that I had just "found" on the street from her house to mine. Being the wise, all-knowing mom she was, she questioned me as to where I *really* got the coin. And of course, I couldn't be caught in a lie, so I continued to lie – again and again and again. Finally, she had enough of the debate and decided to ground me until I told the truth.

About three minutes later, thinking that all I had to do was tell her the truth and I would be free and clear of punishment, I told her that I had actually stolen it from my friend's coin collection. My step-mom, full of a mother's wrath, picked me up and marched me down the street to not only give back the coin, but also tell her I had stolen it and I was very sorry and I would never steal again. And I never did.

Just like God, my step-mom knew I would get into trouble. She loved me enough to discipline me and she knew exactly what to do teach me a valuable lesson. When I was humbled by the experience of admitting the truth, she could then see me as the little girl she loved and cherished.

God loves and disciplines in the same way to you and me. The Lord promised a Redeemer, a Savior to come and redeem His people. Jesus was God's gift for us, a gift that would allow us to communicate with Him, one that would restore our relationship with Him. Our only requirement is that we humbly accept God's free gift.

My step-mom willingly gave me her love. I chose to accept it. I chose to receive it and honor her as my mom. That is all God is looking for, your acceptance of His Son, His greatest love.

Jesus Christ is *the* greatest teacher who ever lived. He is the one from which all-true knowledge and infinite wisdom is learned.

The Bible tells us to demolish all arguments and every pretension that sets itself up against the knowledge of God, and to take every thought captive to the obedience of Christ Jesus (2 Corinthians 10:5). That means we are look to the Word of God to guide us in our daily lives. We need to know what Christ would do in all situations so that we can be obedient and serve Him.

If we are to listen and comply with every other person setting a standard or new way of living, we would become crazy trying to measure up. I praise God that we don't have to do that. He has set His standard in His Word. He does say that we all fall short of His glory, (we can't be perfect) but through His Son, Jesus Christ, we can make mistakes and still be called children of God (Romans 8:1).

We have learned that Jesus Christ is God in a physical body.

John 1:1 says, "In the beginning was the Word, and the Word was with God, and the Word was God. The Word became Flesh (Jesus) and made a dwelling among us. He was in the world, and though the world was made through him, the world did not recognize him…did not receive him" (John 1:10,14).

While Jesus was praying for His disciples, he told God that he has "given them your word and the world has hated them, for they (the believers in Christ) are not of the world any more than I am of the world."

What Jesus was saying is that the people of this world do not have the mind-set of Christ; they are more interested in the materials they can possess than the eternal life that is waiting for them.

Isn't that what has happened to the writers of *The Secret*? Have they not the mind-set of Christ? Have they received the Word and used it for their self-seeking principles, not to point you to God in heaven, but to claim that the universe is the god, that you yourself are a god?

The Secret claims that through the law of attraction we can control the universe; control that universal god with our thoughts and feelings. That idea or philosophy is called pantheism – the belief that God is everything or everyone. *The Secret* is refuting the true identity of God in heaven.

He is a God who is sovereign, omnipotent, and omnipresent, a God who loves, who gives, and who feels. The writers of *The Secret* have given you the possibility that you are in control of your destiny. But Scripture says, "All the days were ordained for me in your book before one of them came to be" (Psalm 139:16).

The responsibility of the people on this earth is not to control the universe, but to spread the love of Christ throughout the world so that we may all share eternal life with Him. We are not to store up possessions for ourselves, but to give and give generously to those in need. We are called to seek wisdom and guidance for our future, not to foolishly spend time wishing for things we don't have.

So often we spin our wheels going nowhere. Isn't it time we find our purpose in the world and use it to serve others?

You won't find your purpose concentrating on the law of attraction, requesting that "magic genie" bring you your dreams on a silver platter. You will only find it on your knees spending quality time listening to your God in heaven who gives you more than you could ever ask, hope, or dream.

Jesus loves us so much; He intercedes for us by praying that we will learn to have a mind-set for Him. Don't you want someone on your side praying for you to have a blessed abundant life? (Remember, God's definition of the "abundant life" is different than that of *The Secret*. God wants you to have peace in Him, knowing that He has you held in the palm of His hand and nothing will pluck you from it. The abundant life with Christ is one filled with joy, love, compassion, kindness, endurance and peace.) You can't control the car in front of you; you can't control your boss; you can't control the life or death of someone; won't you look to the One who can?

Jesus was perfect in every way because he submitted himself to God. Jesus asked for God's provision with every step he took. That is what makes him perfect – God. Near the end of Jesus' life, He prayed to His Father, saying, "I have brought you glory on earth by completing the work you gave me to do" (John 17:4).

Jesus' mission was not self-seeking; it was for you and me so that we might have life for eternity. God placed Jesus in a position of authority to give eternal life so that we would know God, our Father. Jesus' mission was not to glorify Himself so that people would look to Him in awe, but that His actions would lead us to our Heavenly Father.

Jesus said, "Come to me, all you who are weary and burdened, and I will give you rest...learn from me, for I am gentle and humble in heart, and you will find rest for your souls" (Matthew 11:28,29).

Are you ready to rest your soul? You can give all your worries and burdens over to Christ Jesus.

You can simply pray this prayer with me. "Father in heaven, I know I am a sinner. Please forgive me of all my wrongdoings and cleanse me, make me a new spirit within you. Guide me in your way and give me peace. I commit my life to you. In Jesus' name, Amen."

I hope you prayed that prayer. I am praying for you, that your eyes and heart would be opened to receive the Word that the Lord has given you.

MORE TRUTH

Philippians 4:8, "...Brothers, whatever is true, whatever is noble, whatever is right, whatever is pure, whatever is lovely, whatever is admirable-if anything is excellent or praiseworthy-think about such things. Whatever you have learned or received from me-put it into practice. And the God of peace will be with you."

My five-year-old daughter often comes to me in a sad and whiney voice telling me her three-year-old brother told her she was stupid. My reply is usually something like, "Well, sweetheart, are you stupid?" And of course she responds with, "No" in that same sad and whiney tone. To which I will tell her, "Honey, if it's not true, then don't listen to what he said." That has appeared to help her cope with the taunting from her little brother, and although we have the same conversation several times a day, she still wants to be reassured that my answer remains the same.

Isn't that just like our character as adults? What about a time when your husband came home and he took his bad day out on you questioning why dinner isn't ready or why the kids haven't bathed. Have your parents called lately just to nag you for the way you deal with your husband and kids? What about that boss who is never happy with anything you do. Is all of this an indication that you are worthless?

It can certainly make you feel that way. But Philippians 4:8 reminds me to think of what is true. The truth is my husband came home early without notice, my parents don't live here to really see what is going on and I always put forth my best effort at work.

The truth is that I am created in the image of God. I am His princess, an heiress to His throne. I am called a saint and God will not condemn me. God loves me and He has chosen me.

I challenge you to remember what is true the next time someone or something gets you down and feeling gloomy.

Allow me to illustrate this. When you are thinking about that new house you want and your actions are working toward that new house and you ask "the universe" for it, and you believe you will get that new house because you are acting like you already have that new house, you just might get that house.

But realize that because you are not praying to the God in Heaven and you are not seeking His will and guidance for your life, that new house may not be from God. Anything can happen. Your neighbors might be a bad influence on your kids, you may not be able to make the mortgage, and you may end up with more repairs than the house is worth – anything that could go wrong may go wrong.

Now, let's look at this from a godly perspective. Let's say that you are praying to God in heaven, you are being obedient and living in His will. You have faith that the Lord will give you what you ask for and He gives you a new home. All of the same problems and disasters could still happen to you, but the one difference is, you are trusting God to help you through it. You have a different perspective. Because remember, this is God's battle, not yours. You are following in the will of God and He loves you and will meet all of your needs.

Let's look at this scenario from one more angle. You have been praying for a new home, you are being obedient and living in His will. You have faith that the Lord will give you that new home for which you are earnestly praying. And He doesn't give you that new home. You listened to God and did everything He has asked of you, but still no new home. Praise God! Think I am crazy? No, it could be that God has chosen a different, more suitable home for you. Or it could be that where you are now is exactly where He wants you. "My grace is sufficient for you" (2 Corinthians 12:9).

"Many are the plans in a man's heart, but it's the Lord's purpose that prevails," (Proverbs 19:21).

As I was reading the Scriptures God showed me a short, but powerful story that I hope will help you.

In 1 Chronicles 5:18-22, Ezra writes about how the people's success in warfare is credited to their crying out to God. There were three able-bodied tribes equivalent to 44,760 men. Ezra said they were "trained for battle and they waged war against four other tribes. They were helped in fighting them, and God handed all their allies over to them, because they cried out to him during battle. He answered their prayers because they trusted in him...because the battle was God's."

How great is our God! Because we cry to Him and trust Him, He provides our victories! After all, the battle is God's not ours. Do you trust Him?

HOW TO USE THE TRUTH

If you have come this far with me, I pray we have established the very Truth of life.

Rhonda Byrne, however, wants us to see that we are a creator and we must learn from the wisdom and realize that the teachings of the "greatest teachers and avatars" have the essence of the truth of life.

Yes, we can learn from history, from artists, teachers and musicians, but that doesn't mean we hold firmly to their theories and philosophies.

James Ray compares the use of *The Secret* to requesting wishes from the Genie in Aladdin's lamp. He compares the Genie to our sovereign God. Byrne asks us to believe that this "Genie" gives us everything we want.

The problem is if we are really referring to our God in heaven, that isn't true. God doesn't give us everything we want; if He did we would destroy ourselves faster than we already are.

Byrne describes the way to use *The Secret* is through a specific method called, "The Creative Process" and she claims that this process is an example that "was taken from the New Testament in the Bible."

The writers collectively say that the first step is to ask the Universe for what you want. Make a command and the Universe will respond to your thoughts. You should write your requests on paper saying, "I am so happy and grateful now that..." And then explain how you want your life to be in every area. They tell you to be very clear and specific. Otherwise the Universe may send you the wrong order.

Byrne explains that if we are not very clear, the Universe may receive the wrong frequency thus presenting you with mixed results. She compares the request to placing an order in the catalogue; you only have to order once.

The Bible tells you to pray to God, through Jesus Christ. The Holy Spirit is your intercessor – the One who speaks to God those desires, which you cannot verbally express, because the Holy Spirit knows what you need more than you do. He knows how to communicate through you to God to help you with what you really need, not just what you think you need (Romans 8:26).

With the Lord's way, there is no need to worry about finding the "right frequency" or placing the proper order. The Holy Spirit is God's gift to you so that you can be free from worry when giving your requests to God.

The writers tell you not to worry or be concerned with how it will happen, just know that it will.

Nichols tells us that the second step in the Creative Process is to believe with "unwavering faith. Believing in the unseen". She reminds us that when we doubt, that will bring on feelings of disappointment. We should then "take that doubt and shift it. Replace it with unwavering faith," knowing it is already on its way.

Byrne reminds us to "relax, knowing to receive what you ordered [from the catalogue], and get on with your life… When you do that, the law of attraction will powerfully move all circumstances, people, and events, for you to receive." She uses the illustrations of booking a vacation or buying a house, or winning the lottery as examples for the use of faith. You know those things are yours even before you physically receive them because you have already bought them.

She tells you that in order to get to the point of believing, you must begin to make believe. "Be like a child, and make believe. The Genie is responding to your predominant thoughts all the time, not as you ask. Your belief that you have it, that undying faith, is your greatest power."

Truly, as a Christian, your greatest power is Jesus Christ. You are a joint heir with Him (Romans 8:17) and that means you have the same power that Christ has to receive what you have asked for from the Lord.

There isn't a Genie that will magically give you what you order. The Lord loves you so much that He will give you what you need and what He knows is best for you. He doesn't have to determine what style or kind and when He gives, it is perfect, because God cannot be or do otherwise.

According to *The Secret,* the third and final step in The Creative Process is to receive and feel good about it.

Michael Bernard Beckwith said, "This is a feeling Universe. If you just intellectually had something, but you have no corresponding feeling underneath that, you don't necessarily have enough power to manifest what you want in your life. You have to feel it."

Byrne agrees and advises us to "get yourself on the feel good frequency, and you will receive. So feel good now."

The problem with that theory is our emotions have no spiritual influence. Emotions cannot serve as physical criteria of spiritual conditions.

Satan uses our emotions to lead us from the Truth of God; he knows in our humanness, we will flee with our emotions and honor them more than the Lord.

The writers have either misquoted or misrepresented God's Word, or they have only partially explained some truths. They quoted Matthew 21:22, "Whatsoever ye shall ask in prayer, believing, ye shall receive," and Mark 11:24, "What things so ever ye desire, when ye pray, believe that ye receive them, and ye shall have them."

The writers sought Scripture to back up their claims of ask, believe, and receive, but they aren't sending you the right message.

When Jesus said those things, He was talking to his disciples, the people who knew He was God's Son. He wasn't talking to the multitude or just anyone who desires to have more out of life. The reference from which Michael Beckwith spoke came from the parable of "The Withered Fig Tree" found in Matthew 21:18-22 and Mark 11:20-25. Jesus was walking down the road with his disciples and came to a fig tree with nothing on it except leaves. Jesus said to the tree, "May you never bear fruit again!" The fig tree withered immediately. The disciples were so amazed by this and they asked Jesus how he did it. Jesus replied, "I tell you the truth, if you have faith and do not doubt, not only can you do what was done to the fig tree, but also you can say to this mountain, 'Go, throw yourselves into the sea,' and it will be done. If you believe, you will receive whatever you ask for in prayer."

In Mark 11:22, Jesus' reply was, "Have faith in God" (not a Genie). Then the same story told by a different person, Matthew writes in Matthew 21:21, "If you believe (believers in Him, the incarnate Son of God), and do not doubt, you will be able to do what I have done..." So, Christians, believers in Christ Jesus, this is your principle duty. You my friends are required to have faith asking anything in *His Son's* holy name, believing that you will have it and then you may receive it by the power of the Holy Spirit.

The Bible says that when you pray you should ask the Lord's will to be done in your life. There are two different wills of God. The first is God's sovereign will; the second is His permissible will. God's sovereign will is what has been and what remains to be. Nothing can be done without the knowledge of God, without His will to have it done.

This doesn't mean that the Lord wanted you to have a house you can't afford, or that abusive spouse, or the wayward child, but He knows whatever the circumstance is, it will come to pass. This is part of His sovereignty.

The Lord has revealed His will for us in His word, The Bible. We have the power to disobey, but we don't have the right to do so. Therefore, we will be held accountable for our wrongdoings.

God's permissive will is given when we ask for something that may not have been what He would have wanted for us originally. For example, you have had a specific college in mind for your child to attend. This college would be perfect for his major and potentially offer him a lucrative and exciting career. But he has plans to go to a different college, one that may not offer the same benefits as the one you chose. Because you are paying for it, you can say no and allow your perfect will or you can allow him to go to the college of his choice, thereby giving your permissive will.

I think that God allows us to have things the way we want it in order to teach us that ultimately He knows what is best for us. In my adolescent years, I knew God. I knew what He wanted for me and I chose to do things differently. I rebelled against my family, and as a result I was left to fend for myself on the streets. I know this wasn't God's will for me, but He did keep me relatively safe during that time. His sovereign will was to let me live, to allow me to become the adult He wanted me to be, while His permissive will was to let me learn for myself what I needed to, so that I could serve Him in the way I am now.

I have many regrets with the choices I made and I can't get any of that time back. I know God loves me enough to hold my hand through it all.

Rhonda Byrne said, "Trust your instincts. It's the Universe inspiring you. If you have an intuitive or instinctive feeling, follow it, and you will find that the Universe is magnetically moving you to receive what you asked for...Trust the Universe. Trust and believe and have faith."

Do you remember who the prince of this world is? Yes, it's Satan, the angel of light. Here's the bottom line, the Truth. If we do not believe wholeheartedly that Jesus Christ is the Son of God sent to the earth to defeat Satan over death and propitiate for our sins, then our faith lies within ourselves. That is exactly what Satan is trying to do: make you believe you are the creator and giver of your own desires. Remember, the Lord places the desires in our hearts. It is our responsibility to ask the Lord for His perfect will so that we can know those desires are from Him.

Paul explains to us in Romans 4 that we are blessed through righteousness that comes by faith. When we, by faith, accept our gracious Jesus Christ as our Lord over our lives, we are made righteous, made clean from all the unpleasant or terrible things we have done. We are blameless in God's eyes. We can then have hope in our Lord because He promises we can have abundance if we will ask and believe. If we do not waver in unbelief, the Lord will strengthen us in our faith, because God will do what He promises.

We are called to trust, believe and have faith through Jesus knowing He will give us the peace we so desperately need. You can trust your instincts when you put your faith in Him, not the Universe. At that point, God is the one inspiring you. If you have time alone with our Father in Heaven, and are reading and studying His word, and are obedient to his commands, you can then trust His response. Trust and believe and have faith in your Heavenly Father.

When we are justified by faith, through Christ, we are then able to have peace. As Christians, we can have hope and confidence in the glory of God because He created us for His divine purpose, which is to our benefit. So even when we don't have what we want whether it is health, money, or a career, we can still be glad and have hope in the Lord to give us what He knows is best for us.

I have a thirteen year-old daughter. She is bright and full of life. She loves the Lord. She prays and reads His Word and wants to please Him. I received a phone call one day from the police who were waiting with her. They asked me if I would go to the school as soon as possible. About three minutes later, I walked through the door to find two women from Child Protective Services and a police officer that started asking me some daring questions. After about a half an hour, I was asked to leave and she would have to be removed from my home. She was gone for about two months.

You see, my daughter, who was hurting so much inside, cried out for help. She made allegations of sexual abuse in order for the chaos in our home to be settled. The allegations could not be confirmed, but the effects on the family were indescribable.

During this time, I was obviously perplexed and a bit saddened as to what would happen to my family. After all, I had a husband and two other children at home. Because I have been close to the Lord for many years, I knew He had a plan and I was not to worry.

As a result of her sabbatical from home, she and I were able to spend more time together and we are now closer than we ever have been. The relationship between her and her father is growing stronger; they have a deeper understanding of one another. She has developed a better bond with her siblings and my girl has matured.

We know the Lord is good. He does all things for good for those who love Him, who are called according to His purposes (Romans 8:28).

The Secret leads you to believe that we can manipulate the universe into giving us that peace and joy that only comes from our Lord.

If my faith was in this world and I had listened to the chatter from any and every other source, I would have felt distraught and hopeless. I could have made things worse with my words of disdain. I could have been destructive and unproductive. Instead, I chose to hear the words of God. "Be still and know that I Am God."

There are only two choices: faith in this world or faith in Jesus. Jesus said, "I am not of this world… you will die in your sins if you do not believe that I AM who I AM" (John 8:23, 24, GNB). When you call the Universe, believe the Universe will give you what you ask, what you are receiving may not be from God. Conversely, if you call out to God through Jesus, believe Jesus will give you what you ask, what you are receiving is from God.

THE POWER OF PRAYER

God is so good! He is truly amazing! Not only does He give you the Way, the Truth, and Life for eternity, He shows you how to have a relationship with Him along the way.

He teaches us to pray – to communicate with Him so that He can provide for us – so He can show us how much He loves us. In Luke 11:1, the disciples stumbled upon Jesus praying and they were so moved by his intensity and passion that they asked Jesus to teach them how to pray.

He responded with what some know as "The Lord's Prayer." He said, "When you pray, say: 'Our Father in heaven, hallowed be your name, your kingdom come, your will be done on earth as it is in heaven. Give us today our daily bread. Forgive us our debts, as we have also forgiven our debtors. And lead us not into temptation but deliver us from the evil one'" (Matthew 6:9-13).

"Our Father." Jesus began His prayer by addressing God as indicating the Lord desires to have a fatherly relationship with us. Prayer is the way we communicate with Him, the way we develop a relationship with the Father who loves us.

In Mark 14:36, Jesus called His Father, "Abba" meaning daddy. Scripture says we are the clay and He is the potter sculpting us just as we sculpt and mold our children. The very term, "Abba" demonstrates the relationship Jesus had with the Lord, intimate and personal. When we pray, seek the face of our Father in heaven and call out, "Abba."

You and I may have very different relationships with our earthly fathers and thus making this concept an easy reality or a useless venture.

My father loved me and provided for me; he raised me when my mother wouldn't. We were very close for many years and did everything together. He was my comforter, my coach and my playmate. To me, there was no one greater than my daddy. Then during my difficult teen years I became too unruly for him to handle. He felt helpless and as a result, he no longer wanted me around. The end result is that I felt abandoned by him. We haven't spoken in over ten years.

Someone once asked me, "How can you believe God, and love God, when your own father abandoned you when you needed him the most?" My only answer then and now is that I must learn who my God in heaven is and ask him to show me His love.

James Emery White, author of *The Prayer God Longs For,* wrote about his relationship with his daughters. He said, "Back when my daughters were young, when I would come home at the end of a day, they would first want to tell me all about theirs, and then they wanted to play with me. Often this meant fixing my hair. They wanted to put me in rollers, create beads, and put in bows and pins. That kind of intimate interaction could only occur between a father and his daughters. As they worked, they were in heaven".

What a classic illustration of the bond our Father in Heaven desires to have with us.

Romans 8:14-15 gives us a clear understanding of the connection we should be aware of with our Father, "For all who are led by the Spirit of God are children of God. So you should not be cowering, fearful slaves. You should behave instead like God's very own children, adopted into his family - calling Him 'Father, dear Father.'"

We are His children; we can look to Him for everything: guidance, love, support, comfort, discipline, encouragement, and healing (spiritual and physical). Loose all your pretensions, cuddle up into his arms, and let the God of creation love you, comfort you and heal you.

"Our Father, in heaven". Our God is omnipresent and magnificent; He is able to be with us anywhere, anytime.

White, explains that the "most literal reading |of heaven| would be the God in the 'heavens.'" Thus revealing that heaven is every place at one time. "In heaven" reveals to us a sense of magnificence – a place abiding with God, anywhere you cry out to Him. Essentially, you can pray, "Daddy, who is always with me…"

While God can be with us, he can also be separate from us.

White explains, "God comes to us from beyond this world, from outside of this world, bringing that which only he can bring. The heaven of our longing:

eternal, glorified, set apart from sin and decay; the heaven of hope and glory. This is the abode of God, and all that it is flows from all that he is. We don't pray to a lifeless image… We pray to the God of heaven, the God who is all-powerful, all-knowing and ever-present."

Nothing is too big or too challenging for our God in heaven. He is sovereign, magnificent, and all-powerful. He is bigger than any problem you can bring to him. Focus on his ability and not your worth.

"Hallowed be thy name." The very word means revered, sacred, holy, deified. God said in the third commandment, Exodus 20:7, "Do not misuse the name of the Lord your God. The Lord will find anyone guilty who misuses His name" (NIRV). We are not to make anything more holy than our Lord.

When Moses responded to the Lord's command to remove the Israelites from Egypt's captivity, Moses asked the Lord, "When I go to the Israelites and say to them, 'The God of your ancestors sent me to you,' they will ask me, 'What is his name?' So what can I tell them?" God said, "I Am who I Am. You must tell them: 'the one who is called I AM has sent me to you'" (Exodus 3:13,14).

God didn't need any other explanation as to who He is. He is astonishingly holy, astoundingly mighty. He is the I Am.

Praise God when we pray. Tell Him how thankful you are for your salvation. Express your gratitude for His mercy and kindness. When we do this, it will allow us to focus our attention on God. The Psalms have excellent praises to recite to Him. I suggest you look through them and find some that are pertinent to your feelings for Him.

Bill Hybels, author of *Too Busy Not To Pray,* brings out an awesome truth in his book. He notes that God is worthy of our adoration. "How great is the love the Father has lavished on us, that we should be called children of God" (1 John 3:1). Our Father created the numerous stars, the shimmering moon, which gives us light to see at night, the radiant sun for heat and color on earth. He gave you life so that you could live it to its fullest. God is worthy of our worship; offer it up to Him.

"Your kingdom come, your will be done, on earth as it is in heaven." We are constantly asking God to give us things: wealth, love, happiness, health, and relationships. Because God is a sovereign God, He is working to not only have His will be done in us, but in the whole earth.

His purpose must start with us individually so that we can as a whole fulfill His plans throughout the world. We are asking for *His* will, not our own. Sometimes that means having to give up what we want in order to have what is best for us. *The Secret* says that we should keep asking from the Universe that which we want. If we are calling and receiving from the Universe, we defy the true greatness that our sovereign Lord wants for us.

Our life is not our own. We are all an intricate part of God's divine plan. We are here on this earth for relationships, not to ask the Universe for every selfish desire. Since we all have a spirit that resides in us and that spirit will live for eternity, shouldn't we prepare it to spend eternity with and for God?

To illustrate this insight, let's say your seven-year-old daughter asks you for a piece of cake for breakfast and gives you all of the "logical" explanations as to why she should have it. You as her loving, insightful parent will firmly tell her "no." And why? Because you know that cake doesn't provide enough nutrients to get her through till lunch. You know what is best for her. As silly as this example is, I believe it is a perfect example of us when we submit our requests to our heavenly Father. He knows what is best for us, thereby telling us "no" on occasion.

We all ask for things, not knowing what it really is we want. Maybe the child did want cake, but the reality is she was hungry. We are all hungry. God knows better than we do what will satisfy our cravings.

About ten years ago, I moved to West Palm Beach, Florida with my daughter and boyfriend (now husband). My biological mother now lived only an hour away. I thought this was the perfect opportunity to get to know my mother and her family. I hadn't seen her or talked to her in over ten years at that time and we had parted on bad terms. (I was an unruly teenager and she had given up on parenting me.)

Without calling, I knocked on her door and she instantly invited me in. We talked for a little while, debated about who gave up on whom and discussed the missing years between us. By the time I left, I felt like I finally had my mother again. All was forgiven and forgotten – at least that's what I wanted.

The Truth About The Secret

The next few years were rocky at best. We couldn't seem to agree on much. I wanted so much to please her, to make her happy and proud of the person I had become. But the more I tried, the more I felt unworthy of our relationship. Honestly, the only thing we had in common was our love for shopping. So we did that.

Every time I would leave her house, I would cry to my husband about how I just couldn't please her. This of course made my husband angry and consequently we visited less frequently. I prayed and prayed that God would strengthen our relationship. I prayed that He would heal both of our hearts. But to no avail, our relationship hasn't progressed.

You see I was hungry, hungry for parental love. I so desperately needed her to need and want me, but she couldn't. God knew I was hungry. He, however, had a greater plan for me – one I would have never expected! I will tell you about it soon.

James Emery White adds, "Every day a battle rages within human souls between the will of God and the human will. When we approach God in prayer, the battle does not cease; in some ways, it intensifies because then all is on the line. Will we pray for our will or his? Will the prayer be an effort to convince God to grant my desires, or for him to plant his desires in me? When I ask for his guidance, will I listen? Do I even desire to? We should not be casual about this or underestimate the arduous nature of the task. It is one thing to acknowledge a king; it's quite another to allow yourself to be ruled."

Remember that God's will is good, perfect and pleasing (Romans 12:2). Pray for His will in us as well and for the kingdom to come.

"Give us this day our daily bread." By praying this way, we are submitting ourselves to the sovereignty of God. We trust Him to give us what we need – we are not doing what we want and saying, "Well if God doesn't want me to have this, then He will stop me from trying to have it." I believe that is a cop-out. When we ask for our daily bread, we are dependant on Him to do just that.

Often when I pray, I ask Him for guidance in my day, to lead me down His perfect path. I ask Him for wisdom when dealing with my children. I ask for discernment to make the right choices. I ask for these each day with the full belief that He will give them to me. By doing this daily, I know that what I am doing is the will of God.

Philippians 4:6,7 states, "Do not be anxious about anything, but in everything, by prayer and petition, with thanksgiving submit your requests to God. And the peace that transcends all understanding will guard your hearts and minds in Christ Jesus."

Give to God all of your worries, concerns and troubles. Expect him to provide because He says He will. If you need a miracle, ask without reservation. James 4:2 clearly states, "You have not, because you ask not." Believe that God will do what He says He will do.

God is faithful; He won't let you down. God's word tells us, "For I know the plans I have for you, plans to prosper you and not harm you, plans to give you hope and a future" (Jeremiah 29:11). Doesn't that give you goose bumps? It does me. The Lord will guide your steps.

A great Psalmist with pure devotion for the Lord poetically phrased, "Your Word is a lamp for my feet and a light for my path." Proverbs 3:5-6 states, "Trust in the Lord with all your heart, lean not on your own understanding, in all your ways acknowledge Him and He will make your paths straight."

> "If we stay focused on Him, instead of our circumstances, we will grow spiritually."
> Oswald Chambers

"Forgive us our debts as we forgive our debtors." The word, "debt" here can also be translated as sin. "Lord, please forgive our sins." *The Strong Dictionary* translates "debt" as a moral fault. Therefore, a sin is anything that isn't truth: a white lie, looking at someone in lust, cheating on a test or taxes, being rude, self-centered or selfishness.

The trouble with sin is that it keeps us from being inline with God. Scriptures say that unconfessed sin divides the communication with Him. The Bible also says that we have *all* sinned and have fallen short of God's glory (Romans 3:23, emphasis mine).

Because we are all sinners, and God hates sin, we need to confess our sins to Him in order for Him to hear our prayers.

Picture this: your best friend didn't do something she said she was going to do and you were dependent on her to do it. You then retaliated in anger and swearing but never apologized. The next day you met her for your weekly coffee date, expecting everything to be okay. Do you think she would hear what you are saying or do you think she would be so hurt that she couldn't focus on your words? This is how it is with God. He needs you to open the lines of communication by acknowledging your faults, asking Him to forgive you, and help you to live according to His will.

The second part of this section of prayer also requires us to forgive others. This means we are required to forgive them whether or not they have asked for it. To forgive is a matter of *your* heart, not theirs.

The easiest way for me to understand this concept is to look at it from a "sin" perspective. We have established that there is sin in this world as a result of Adam and Eve's choices. And I can't do anything about the sinful nature in another person. Until the Lord does His work with us on a particular subject, our transgression continues to affect not only others, but also ourselves. Sometimes we can't help sinning nor do we know that what we are doing is offending others. Often times, we simply don't care thus producing more sin.

I can choose to become embittered by this or I can choose to forgive the sin in them. If God can forgive the sin in me, all the garbage and suffering I have created, I must find it in my heart to forgive the other person's sin. Often times, although we are in control of our sin, it is the sinful nature taking over our choices, thus producing a snowball effect for which we cannot stop until confronted with our iniquity.

My mother's heart is hardened. She made some choices in her life for which she hasn't forgiven herself. I could be angry with her for those choices, I could be resentful because she lost hope in me when I was a teenager, or I could be offended by our lack of connection, but I choose to forgive. I love her because she is my mother, because she gave me life. Until God works with her heart, I cannot change her. All I can do is forgive.

> For if you forgive men their trespasses, your heavenly Father will also forgive you. But if you do not forgive men their trespasses, neither will your father in heaven forgive your trespasses. Matthew 6:14-15

"And lead us not into temptation, but deliver us from the evil one." When we ask the Lord to keep us from temptation, 1 Corinthians 10:13 reminds us that, "No temptation has seized us except what is common to man. And God is faithful; he will not let you be tempted beyond what you can bear. But when you are tempted, he will also provide a way out so that you can stand up under it."

Simply put, if we want to serve Christ Jesus, if we want to do the right thing, if we want our Lord to be proud of us and we don't think we can withstand the temptation put in front of us, call upon the name of the Lord and He will provide a way for you to be obedient to Him. Take heart knowing you can do all things through Christ who empowers you!

Pray without ceasing. Jesus prayed in everything He did. Luke 5:16 tells us that before He taught, before He healed people, He prayed; Jesus often withdrew to lonely places and prayed. Jesus knew that He alone couldn't heal and teach, but only through His father could these things be done. He went out to a mountainside to pray and spent the night praying to God just before He chose His twelve disciples (Luke 6:12).

In Luke 18:1, Jesus told His disciples to pray and not give up. We are commanded to pray that we will not fall into temptation. Just before He was about to be arrested, Jesus prayed earnestly as He was in anguish about the coming events.

In the book of John, Jesus set the example of praying for others, praying for His disciples, and praying for Himself.

Jesus trusted God in everything. He trusted God with His reputation, His future, His timing and His provision. Can you? Through prayer and obedience, God will work miracles through you. Can you trust Him to do what He has promised?

If you want more out of life, if you want your dreams to come true, pray. Pray to God in Jesus' name, through the Holy Spirit and these things will be given to you.

When you do pray, the enemy will begin to harass you. He isn't used to you speaking your thoughts aloud through the Holy Spirit. He won't like it and therefore try to shake up what little faith you have tried to exude. Remember, God is in control; He has given you weapons to fight against the enemy.

It's called the Armor of God.

Ephesians 6:10-18, "...be strong in the Lord and in his mighty power. Put on the full armor of God so that you can take your stand against the devil's schemes. For our struggle is not against flesh and blood, but against the rulers, against the authorities, against the powers of this dark world and against the spiritual forces of evil in the heavenly realms.

"Therefore put on the full armor of God so that when the day of evil comes, you may be able to stand your ground, and after you have done everything to stand. Stand firm then, with the belt of truth buckled around your waist, with the breastplate of righteousness in place, and with your feet fitted with the readiness that comes from the gospel of peace. In addition to all this, take up the shield of faith with which you can extinguish all the flaming arrows of the evil one. Take the helmet of salvation and the sword of the Spirit which is the Word of God."

To illustrate, because you are being obedient to the Lord, Satan will do everything in his power to deceive you and cause you to fall away from God. Picture yourself in a duel with your archenemy (in this case it's Satan). You are suited in armor with a breastplate, a belt, a helmet and a sword. You are dressed and ready for battle, ready to conquer any evil thing that comes in your path.

Your archenemy will come first at your waist because it is the largest area and a potential weak spot. You are to take your stand with the belt of Truth, which is your character, the person God created you to be – strong in Him and in the power of His might. Your archenemy will then stab at your chest with his next offense. Use your breastplate of righteousness, knowing you have been justified through Christ to take a stand against the devil and his schemes.

Because you have heard the gospel, the Truth of Jesus Christ, God gives you peace to know that what you are doing for Him is the right thing to do. Plant your feet firmly on that peace which the Lord has given. Raise your shield of unwavering faith, knowing the Lord is the winner, knowing you are an heir to Him and that you will win this battle and extinguish all flames thrown by your enemy.

The helmet of salvation will have washed you clean. You don't have to worry about the past mistakes you have made. Don't let the enemy bring up those things, which have been erased from you. Just because you have failed in your fighting before, doesn't mean you will loose this time, because you have the undying faith in Christ. Let the helmet give you deliverance from your nemesis.

Finally, use your double-edged sword to fight back. The sword is the word of God, which is living and active. It penetrates your enemy even to dividing its soul and spirit, joints and marrow (Hebrews 4:12). The Lord then declares you the winner!

Remember, the Lord blesses obedience!

"And Satan trembles when he sees the weakest saint on his knees." William Cowper

The Lord gives wisdom. James, the half-brother of Jesus, wrote, "If any of you lacks wisdom, he should ask God, who gives generously to all without finding fault, and it will be given to him (James 1:5). James was referring to anyone who was facing a trial, conflict, or crisis in his or her life. Pray to God who gives wisdom. Do not ask with doubt, but with all certainty that the Lord will provide - because He says He will.

It is impossible for God to lie (Hebrews 6:18). "When we ask anything according to God's will, he hears us. And if we know that he hears us – whatever we ask – we know that we have what we asked of Him" (1 John 5:14-15).

God is one God revealed as, God the Father, God the Son, and God the Holy Spirit (Genesis 1:1). We are taught to pray to the Father, but in the name of Jesus, through the Holy Spirit. We must first have a relationship with Jesus before we can have access to the Father. The Holy Spirit then intercedes for us. Remember, we just learned that the Spirit is the One who speaks to God those desires, which you cannot verbally express, because the Holy Spirit knows what you need more than you do. He knows how to communicate through you to God to help you with what you really need, not just what you think you need (Romans 8:26).

Isn't God awesome! He is your friend and your father. He wants the best for you and He wants you to have life abundantly, so much that He has given you His Word so that you may study and know that He is the one, true God; the giver of life and joy in that life.

Let God be your Father and when you do, praise Him for His mighty miracles.

It can be easy and so very human of us to reduce prayer to a simple formula. But the truth is, we are called to pray. So wherever you are, please pause for a moment. Bow your head, close your eyes, and ask Christ to be the Lord over your life. Let him be your guide, your comforter and your answer for living life abundantly.

If you haven't already, pray out loud, "Lord, I am a sinner. Forgive me of my transgressions. I turn my life over to you. I want you to come into my heart and guide me, be the Lord of my life. Thank you for saving me. In your Son Jesus' name, Amen."

"Prayer is the blueprint for a successful life."
Joyce Meyer

GOD'S POWERFUL PROCESS

Dr. Joe Vitale realizes that "people feel stuck or imprisoned or confined by their current circumstances." The fabrication transpired when he said, our "current reality will begin to change as a result of beginning to use *The Secret*."

Application of *The Secret* is not what will change our current reality. What is true is the way we live now is a direct reflection of our thoughts that have been imbedded since childhood. For example, some of us intentionally treat our spouses in the same way our parents treated each other, while some of us vow to never be the way our parents were to one another, but the truth is, until we become aware of our intentions, we won't ever be able to make the right decisions.

Rhonda Byrne said, "Your current reality or your current life is a result of the thoughts you have been thinking. All of that will totally change as you begin to change your thoughts and feelings." Yes, Ms.

The Truth About The Secret

Byrne, that is true, but it is important to know what we should be thinking.

So how do we change those thoughts and feelings?

Thoughts and feelings come and go. Thoughts can be deceiving – you and I know that from experience alone. Do you remember any time in your life when you thought something was true when the reality wasn't at all the way your mind perceived it? How did it turn out? Thoughts will do that to you.

My step-mom and my father divorced when I was eleven years old. She was the only mom I knew, for she and my dad had dated since I was three. For a couple of months, I visited her on the weekends. One particular weekend we entered her apartment and she walked straight to the answering machine. There was a message that said, "Hi there, it's Michael. I had a great time last night; I hope to do it again soon. Call me. Bye." Immediately, I tensed up and felt as if my father had already been replaced, but I didn't ask her about the message.

Our weekend went well as usual – until our car ride home to my dad's house. What I remember her telling me is: "Stephanie, I love you. I will always be here for you. You can always call me if you need me, but I can't continue to see you anymore. This is unfair to your dad for us to continue these visits. It hurts him and me too much. But if you ever need me, I will be a phone call away."

I never called her. She too had abandoned me. At least that is how I felt.

Seventeen years later, after years of praying to God for the relationship with my biological mother to work, He gave me Brenda – my step-mom. She wrote me a letter telling me about her life now and that she would like to hear from me. After some time and phone conversations, she came to visit me.

After she had settled in, she opened her suitcase and pulled out letters I had written to her as a child. She made for me a scrapbook of our life together and gave me the quilt she had made for the bed she had saved for me on the nights I would sleep over. She handed me a shirt that she kept from our first vacation together. She had loved me. She didn't want to loose me – but I didn't hear it that way.

Brenda and I talked about that dreadful day, she reminded me of what she really said. She reminded me of the bedroom she decorated for me. She made the quilt specially for the bed I would have slept in when I came to visit. What she had really said was she wanted me to want to see her. She didn't want to be selfish and keep me from my dad. I needed to initiate the visitations. She never did abandon me; she loved me. She was waiting on me for seventeen years and I never knew it.

Your feelings can deceive you in the same way. I once heard someone say, "Life is a choice, and your feelings will follow."

I train for a marathon about once a year. The training process is the same each time. In the beginning, it is so hard for me to even get outside and take that first step towards the first thirty minute run. But, I make the choice to set out my clothes the night

The Truth About The Secret

---

before, I set the alarm to wake up an hour earlier than usual and the morning of, I head out the door. I don't feel like waking up, I don't feel like running in the heat, but if I don't get out there, I will not ever accomplish my goal of finishing the race I set out to run.

We all have choices to make. The way we go about making our decisions is the key to success in all we do.

2 Chronicles 6:30, Solomon tells us that our thoughts come from our hearts. Scripture says, "The heart is deceitful among all things, and desperately wicked who can know it" (Jeremiah 17:9). Consequently, our thoughts are deceiving.

I can think about it being too early to get up. I can think about how getting out of bed an hour early and running will affect my performance for the day as a mother of three kids. But those thoughts don't serve me.

How then do we know when our thoughts are truthful? Only God can help you discern the Truth from a lie.

King David knew this when he prayed, "Search me O God, try me and know my thoughts and see if there be any wicked way in me, and lead me in the way everlasting" (Psalm 139:23,24). David wanted God's approval; he knew the only way to live in the will of God was to have the Lord search his heart to find even a hint of wrongdoing, and then correct it.

In the situation of whether or not to get out the door, I truly believe that if I prayed for God to find the wickedness in me, He would say that it is my lack of faith in His ability to sustain me throughout the day. Then I must get outside, run by tail off, and have faith that God will put me on autopilot for the rest of the day.

When God sees you, His child, He sees you in the perfect way He created you. He doesn't see any of your flaws. He knows what you are capable of, both good and bad, but He can only see you through His Son, Jesus. That is why it is so important to repent of any wrongdoing so that you may have the favor of God. I must cast aside all doubts of being a successful marathoner because God already sees me as one.

James Ray realized that people limit themselves by saying, "This is who I am." They just accept what they have as what they will always have or what they are as what they will always be. He is right when he stated, "That's not who you are; that's the residual outcome of your past thoughts and actions."

Instead of limiting yourself to what you are now, rely on your heavenly Father to show you who you are. After all, He knew you before He formed you in your mother's womb (Jeremiah 1:5). Whatever you think of yourself ask God to show you the Truth. "Take every thought captive to the obedience of Christ" (2 Corinthians 10:5). That means to ask Jesus what He would do – what the Bible says about this particular situation.

When you think you are incapable, place your capabilities in Christ. Remember, you can do all things through Christ who gives you strength (Philippians 4:13). When you are feeling blue based on a lack of self-worth, remember that you are "fearfully and wonderfully made" (Psalm 139:14).

And when you act out of selfish ambition, remember not to be hard on yourself. God forgives. For when you sin, confess it to God and He is faithful to forgive you (1 John 1:9). Because God sees you flawless, you can look at yourself through God's eyes and through Him, you will be able to achieve anything.

The Secret explains that the expression of gratitude is part of the powerful process that will bring more of what you want from the Universe. While the writers may be heading in the right direction on this subject, remember, it's not the Universe that gives, it's God who gives.

Dr. Joe Vitale encourages us to write down things for which we are grateful. James Ray agrees; he reveals his morning ritual through this process. He said he starts every day with a "Thank you." While he moves through his morning, he verbally expresses his gratitude for all things.

The Secret says that we should be in a practice of thinking about things for which we are thankful instead of things we wish we didn't have. God would agree. Scripture says on a number of occasions to give thanks in everything.

My concern for you is that you do not simply thank the air or the Universe for giving you that which you are grateful, but that you would thank your Father in heaven who knows you well enough to please you and to do what is best for you. The

Bible tells us that every good and perfect gift comes from God above (James 1:17).

In 1 Thessalonians 5:18, Paul writes, "In everything give thanks; for this is the will of God in Christ Jesus for you."

I know first hand how difficult that is. I can certainly thank God when all things are going well or if they are just going, but to give thanks when I need new tires at $300 each makes me cringe. My step-mom would remind me to think of what I am thankful for in this situation and give my praise to the Lord. I will in turn say, "Thank you Lord that I can afford the new tires" or "Thank you Lord for the vehicle you have given me to drive" or "Thank you Lord in advance for providing me with the money to pay for these new tires." I believe that is the kind of thanksgiving He wants from us. The Lord knows times will be difficult, but He wants us to know He is there to help us along the way.

The Apostle Paul was a man who had suffered a great deal of persecution from the Jewish people. He was commanded by God to reveal the Truth of Jesus Christ. God also told Paul that he would suffer for Christ namesake. Paul was shipwrecked three times, beaten several times and jailed many more times. After a great deal of persecution, Paul still told the Philippians that he had "learned the secret so that any where, any time, I am content, whether it be a full stomach or hunger, whether I have too much or too little; for I have the strength to face all conditions by the power Christ gives me" (Philippians 4:12,13 GNB).

This is how the Lord wants us to know Him. He wants our hearts to be satisfied with Him and Him alone. Give your thanks and gratitude to your Father in heaven, not to the empty air or the depraved Universe.

The Secret includes the process of visualization in their "Creative Process." They use the belief system that you can create pictures in your mind and that will emit frequencies into the Universe that will eventually manifest itself. "The law of attraction will take hold of that powerful signal and return those pictures back to you, just as you saw them in your mind" (Rhonda Byrne).

The writers tell you to picture yourself behind the wheel of a car; visualize your hands wrapped around the steering wheel.

Dr. Joe Vitale says, "This is such a holographic experience – so real in this moment – that you don't even feel as if you need the car, because it feels like you have it already." He continues, "If you turn it over to the Universe, you will be surprised and dazzled by what is delivered to you. This is where magic and miracles happen." Dr. Vital also reminds us that we must possess happy feelings about what we are visualizing.

Marci Shimoff says, "The only difference between people who live in this way, who live in the magic of life, and those who don't is that the people who live in the magic of life have habituated ways of being. They've made a habit of using the law of attraction, and magic happens with them wherever they go because they remember to use it. They use it all the time, not just as a one-time event."

If that is true, why hasn't my husband won the lottery? He has habitually bought the ticket with happy feelings about winning. He has envisioned himself pulling up his winning numbers online, driving the seemingly endless four hours to pick up the money, feeling the money in his hands, and placing it in the bank. He has already set up the tithing plan, charity plan, prepared for investments, and decided which vacation we would take first. My husband has the blueprints for the house he will build and he knows where we will build it. This plan has been in effect since we were married six years ago. And he is happy about it. Why hasn't the lottery money manifested itself for us?

It is true; the vision you look at the longest becomes the strongest. For example, when you drive down the highway at 80 mph, you can briefly look to the left or to the right to see what is around you, but you have to keep your focus on the road ahead. If you look to the left or right too long, your automatic response is to steer the car in that direction. The same is true when you are running. If you want to run straight, you have to look straight ahead. Therefore, if you are focusing on making more money, you will automatically do what it takes to make more money: get a second job, a third job, cut down on expenses, etc. If you are focusing on how much debt you have, it is easy to fall into that slump of depression, which can bring you to more debt.

Paul reminds us to stay the course. Continue forward to the prize that Jesus has already won for us. Focus your minds on heavenly things, not earthly things, which pass away with the wind. Heaven is eternal; earth is limited. The only way to do that is by keeping your mind, soul, and heart focused on Him.

You must pray knowing God will provide, visualize that answered prayer and take the action necessary to fulfill that prayer. Visualize God's plan for you, visualize eternity, and visualize Truth. If you really want a miracle, turn it over to our Father in heaven, not the Universe.

WAITING ON GOD

God has an ultimate design for your life. He wants to bless you more than you could ever ask, hope or dream. His requirement is that you become His child, reliant on Him solely, through His Son Christ Jesus. He wants you to have a relationship with Jesus. That means to connect with Him in thought, heart and spirit. God loves you unconditionally, without your perfect performance. He only wants you to need Him, to desire Him and His will for your life.

When you have humbled yourself and accepted Christ Jesus to be your Lord, you must then seek His guidance and will. That doesn't mean to get down on your knees and spill out your demands from Him and become anxious when He isn't giving it to you right away. We must be patient and wait for His perfect timing. He commands us to "Be still and know that I am God" (Psalm 46:10).

We must do our part and give our best so that we can bring glory to God. We must be obedient to do all that He asks of us. Sometimes we try to analyze Him and get so caught up with what makes sense to us that we fail to do what God has asked us to do. Remember God's way is perfect (Romans 12:2).

If you do not get that which you have asked, it may not be God's will, but never give up in your faith that God will provide a better way. The Apostle Paul tells us that distress produces perseverance; perseverance, character; and character, hope.

Oswald Chambers said, "Perseverance is our supreme effort of refusing to believe that our hero is going to be conquered." We must stand strong in the Lord knowing He will do what He says He will do, first because God cannot lie, and second "because we have kept His command to persevere (Revelation 3:10).

Persevering in walking by faith knowing that God too is faithful to complete His promises. Walking by faith will produce character – the result of who you really are. I believe the Lord wants to test our commitment to Him. After all, do you really want a disloyal person doing battle for you? When God has revealed our true character and we have proven ourselves to be faithful to Him, He will then use you to serve His purpose.

Character produces hope. Hope is the expectation in something that is uncertain or unknown. The Lord doesn't want us to hope that we can have a million dollars or hope that we can stay healthy. He wants us to have hope in Him, in His coming, in His redemption of our souls. When God has tested and approved us for His work, He will equip you with the power and strength to do all things through Christ. Place your hope in the Lord.

God does want to bless you beyond your wildest dreams. Your responsibility is to give yourself to Him. The stuff of this world is not what is important. These too will pass, but the spirit that resides in you is eternal. If you are going to do something for yourself, do something with your soul, your spirit. Give it to your heavenly Father so that He can bless you more than you could ever dream, hope or imagine.

THE TRUTH ABOUT MONEY

Rhonda Byrne said, "To attract money, you must focus on wealth."

She believes that if you focus on the abundance of money, the Universe will bring it to you. She encourages us to play mind games of having wealth. The more we feel good about having money, the more money we will attract.

Dr. Joe Vitale says to intend money coming into your life. "Declare what you would like to have from the catalogue of the Universe. 'I would like to have twenty-five thousand dollars, unexpected income, within the next thirty days.'" Believe it and have good thoughts about it.

I encourage you again to take these thoughts and ideas to the obedience of Christ. What does He say about money?

Upon researching this issue in the Bible, I was reminded that God is in control – even in our finances. He has given us responsibility with the money He gives, while also accepting some responsibility

Himself. As Believers, we are required to search His Word to find out exactly which responsibility belongs to whom.

Did you know that Jesus spoke about the issue of money almost more than any other subject? There are over 2,350 verses in the Bible on the subject of money.

I believe that God knew the possible defeat the love of money could bring. He knows that greed will lead to destruction, so Scripture carefully and extensively explains where money comes from, what it is to be used for, and how we should use it.

King Solomon, the man to whom God promised riches said, "If you long for money, you will never be satisfied; if you long to be rich, you will never get what you want. It is useless" (GNB). 2 Chronicles 1:7-12 explains that God wanted to bless King Solomon. The Lord said to him, "Ask for whatever you want me to give you." Solomon replied, "Give me wisdom and knowledge, that I may lead these people, for who is able to govern this great people of yours?" God said to Solomon, "Since this is your heart's desire and you have not asked for wealth, riches or honor, nor for the death of your enemies and since you have not asked for a long life, but for wisdom and knowledge to govern my people over whom I have made you king, therefore wisdom and knowledge will be given you. And I will also give you wealth, riches and honor, such as no king who was before you ever had and none after you will have."

After all the Lord gave to King Solomon, he still reminded us that many things are "meaningless" in this world, but the one thing he proclaimed to be true is that our reverence and adoration for God is the purpose for which we were created.

The Apostle Paul struck a chord when he asserted, "For the love of money is a root of all kinds of evil" (1Timothy 6:10a). He explains, "Some have been so eager to have it that they have wandered away from the faith and have broken their hearts with many sorrows. But you, man of God, avoid all these things. Strive for righteousness, godliness, faith, love, endurance, and gentleness" (1 Timothy 6:10b, 11 GNB).

Jesus said, "It is hard for a rich man to enter the kingdom of heaven...it is easier for a camel to go through the eye of a needle than for a rich man to enter the kingdom of God" (Matthew 19:24). Jesus wasn't saying that rich people couldn't go to heaven, but that if man values his money or his prosperity more than eternal life, then the result is eternal death. That rich man needs to realize he has prosperity because the Lord has allowed it. His riches didn't come from the Universe and his good feelings of having money.

God's Word says, "Both riches and honor come from you...all things come from You [God]" (1 Chronicles 29:12-14). The Lord asks us to give our attention to Him before anything else, and when we do that, all the rest will be given to us, but according to His riches not our own (Matthew 6:33 & Philippians 4:19).

"A dreadful thing is the love of money! It disables both eyes and ears, and makes men worse to deal with than a wild beast, allowing a man to consider neither conscience nor friendship nor fellowship nor salvation." John Chrysostom

"Let us not ask of the Lord deceitful riches, nor the good things of this world, nor transitory honors; but let us ask for light." Gregory Nazianzen

The Secret tells you, "the only reason any person does not have enough money is because they are blocking money from coming to them with their thoughts."

The reason people may or may not have wealth is based on their faithfulness to God and His money. *The Secret* focuses on thinking you can have prosperity; believing and confessing it without any doubts and you will become wealthy.

Jesus asks in Luke 16:11, "…if you have not been trustworthy in handling worldly wealth, who will trust you with true riches?"

Isn't it possible that the reason one may not have enough money is because he or she hasn't been faithful with it?

"Nothing I am sure has such a tendency to quench the fire of religion as the possession of money." C., Ryle, J.

David Schirmer said, "When it comes to creating wealth…it's all about how you think."

If we decide that wealth is simply about how we think, then we have put our ideas in a box from which we draw this idea or that and take on that which we have drawn. We have to place our hearts and minds in Truth, not a box of ideas that will lead us down a path of superfluous dreams. Come on, do you really think that by saying, "I am a money magnet" that money will just draw itself to you? The only way you will receive money everyday is if you work for it. Please don't subject yourself to man made wisdom and philosophies.

Rhonda Byrne stumbled upon a glimpse of Truth when she said, "Giving is a powerful action to bring more money into your life."

The untruth, however, is what she implied when she said it. "By the law of attraction, the Universe opens up and floods vast amounts of money back to them – multiplied."

The truth is, God offers a promise in Malachi 3:10: "The Lord said, 'Bring the whole tithe into the storehouse, that there may be food in my house. Test me in this, and see if I will not throw open the floodgates of heaven and pour out so much blessing that you will not have room enough for it.'"

This is the one place in all of Scripture, the Lord commands us to test Him. And that's a blessing I am willing to work for, aren't you?

The Bible teaches us that we will be rewarded in Heaven for the things we have done on earth. We will receive crowns according to the good we have shown on earth. When we give to the Lord, for the Lord, we

The Truth About The Secret

are sharing a bit of ourselves as well as our faith with those in need.

The blessings He is talking about may not be a monetary blessing. It may be something that warms your soul. The Lord might answer a specific prayer that you have persistently prayed over. Or you may one day meet the people you served as a result of your sacrifice. The blessing from that, to me, is indescribable.

The Secret tells you to "give money in order to bring more out of it into your life. When you are generous with money and feel good about sharing it, you are to say, 'I have plenty.'"

The Bible does teach us to "be generous and share your food with the poor, you will be blessed for it" Proverbs 22:9 (GNB). Not only are we required to give a tithing, but we should also be giving to those in need. These are not decrees given so that you may selfishly and monetarily prosper, but so that your hearts will be blessed.

Remember to serve our Father in Heaven who gives you the means to provide for the less fortunate; your Father will then bless your soul.

> "It is what we get by the soul that makes us rich." Henry Ward Beecher

The Secret says to "tip the balance of your thoughts to wealth. Think wealth." However, Jesus warns us in Luke 12:15, "Watch out and guard yourselves from every kind of greed; because your true life is not made up of the things you own, no matter how rich you may be."

Proverbs 17:16 decrees, "Of what use is money in the hand of a fool, since he has no desire to get wisdom." Our Father invites us to ask for wisdom and he promises if we seek first His kingdom, His heart's desire for us, the rest will be given (Matthew 6:33).

The Lord has a specific plan for you and His money.

The Truth is simple. Confess that you have made poor choices or that you haven't followed God's plan. Surrender to His will and make His plan your daily habit and watch your finances grow. You must acknowledge that everything under the sun belongs to God (This includes money). (1 Chronicles 29:11) Recognize the Truth that when you put God first in your life, (and your finances), honor His commands, He will provide for you. The Lord requires us to be faithful stewards of our money (1 Corinthians 4:2). He will bless us or discipline us according to our obedience or lack there of (Matthew 25:14-30).

THE TRUTH ABOUT RELATIONSHIPS

Marie Diamond, a Feng Shui consultant and speaker said, "*The Secret* means that we are creators of our Universe, and that every wish that we want to create will manifest in our lives. Therefore, our wishes, thoughts and feelings are very important because they will manifest."

She applies this philosophy in the area of relationships as well. She instructs you to paint the picture of what you want (not what you don't want) in order to achieve your ideal relationship.

Rhonda Byrne suggests whatever it is we want from life, we should be sure our actions don't contradict our desires. In addition, Byrne reminds us, "Our thoughts create the words we speak, the feelings we feel, and our actions. Actions are particularly powerful, because they are thoughts that have caused us to act."

According to *The Secret,* we should put ourselves first in any relationship. Dr. John Gray says, "you become the solution for you…give more to yourself…now you can overflow in giving."

Rhonda Byrne points out, "Many of us were taught to put ourselves last, and as a consequence we attracted feelings of being unworthy and undeserving…unless you fill yourself up first, you have nothing to give anybody…attend to your joy first." She continues, "You must change your focus and begin to think about all the things that are wonderful about you. Look for the positives in you. As you focus on those things, the law of attraction will show you more great things about you."

The only thing we need to fill ourselves up with is the love of Christ. "Since God loved us, we also ought to love one another" (1 John 4:11).

When we look to the positives in ourselves from a worldly perspective, what we see is a result of pride. We are told to humble ourselves before the Lord, knowing that what we do and who we have become is a result of His mercy and grace. When we do good deeds for others, we must do them because we love the Lord, not because it makes us look good. That would be prideful. Instead, with humility, we should obtain self-worth by honoring the Lord with praise and sacrifice for Him and through a relationship with Him.

When you and I seek to have a relationship with Jesus, He will guide us in doing things we never thought we could. He will test our own limits and our will. Through the work of Christ, we will develop a sense of self-worth that is unexplainable.

I briefly talked about the absence of my father during my teen years. And although my mother was alive, she was also absent throughout my life. She and her husband raised my older and younger half-sisters, but not me. I could feel like I am a worthless, rejected child, one who isn't worthy of living or of having a family of my own. I could think that I am not capable of raising competent, God-loving children. But instead, I have chosen to look at who I am through God's eyes.

He says I am His child, who is forgiven and saved by grace through my faith in Him. I have been justified by Christ, who died for me. I can cast all my cares on him and I am one who has overcome adversity. I can do all things through Christ who gives me the strength necessary to achieve the dreams He has for me.

As a result of my relationship with the Lord, I have a family who loves and serves God. The Lord has also given me back a mother (my step-mom) who loves me and who has prayed for me over those disheartening years as a teenager and young adult.

Jesus Christ set the example of real love. He sacrificed His life for you so that you could have eternal life. Everything He did on this earth was of benefit to you; it was not to benefit Him. Jesus' sole purpose for His life was to save yours. He didn't do that by thinking of himself first. He looked to God, His Father, for guidance.

Rick Warren, author of *The Purpose Driven Life* and *Better Together* said, "Life is all about love and developing relationships – with God and with other people." He continues, "Real love is placing the need of others before your own. It is making your problem, my problem. It is giving to another without any guarantee of getting anything back. It is giving others what they need, not what they deserve. Although love can create intense feelings, love is not a feeling. It is a choice, an action, a way of behaving, a commitment. Love is sacrificing for others."

My husband has an amazing ability of demonstrating his love for me. This one specific time, I felt particularly blue. I went through my days just going through the motions, not knowing exactly what was wrong. I didn't ignore my family in the traditional sense, but I only answered them with the little energy I had. My husband could have been angry, (which is a common emotion for him), or he could have told me about myself, but instead he called my step-mom and asked her to visit. He told her I needed some "mother-daughter" time and it was imperative she come right away. Just the thought of nestling with my mom made me feel like my old self again. She was here the following month. My husband gave me exactly what I needed, certainly not what I deserved.

The Truth is you must change your focus and begin to think of the wonderful things about the Lord. As you focus on Him, the more great things He will show you. God places His love in us so that He can love through us.

Proverbs 3:5,6 states, "Trust in the Lord with all your heart, and lean not on your own understanding; in all your ways acknowledge Him and He will direct your paths."

The Lord instructs us to trust in Him, not in any law of attraction. We are to put the Lord first, not ourselves. When we seek the counsel of the Lord in our relationships, He will provide the perfect relationships for us, whether an acquaintance, a friend or a marriage partner. He does this because of His love for us. He wants us to have His best, that's why He chooses our perfect mate.

The Secret suggests that if you think of the kind of person you want to have in your life, then you will attract that person. It says you must have good feelings about relationships and about yourself so that you can attract the same to you.

The only time we should be focusing on ourselves is when it comes to the matter of the heart and our relationship with Jesus Christ. Applying the love of Christ is the secret to relationships. When we can learn to love Jesus, we will learn to love each other. Since love is a choice, an act of will, any good feelings we have without love are simply void. Jesus' standard of love is personal. He reached out to the undeserving, looking past their faults and into the desperate needs of their hearts.

The Secret teaches that we must learn to love ourselves before we can love anyone else. Rhonda Byrne encourages us to look at the positive attributes we possess and start thinking good thoughts.

Lisa Nicholas reminds us not to let others create our happiness. The joy lies within us and we should celebrate that.

But what we should celebrate as children of God is who we are in Him. The very fact that God himself has chosen me to be His child, and has prepared a special room in His heavenly kingdom just for me is enough for me to share His love with others. What about you?

Because I am a child of God, He says I am a pleasure to Him (Ephesians 1:5). I am blessed by Him (Genesis 1:28). I have a purpose, life and peace, power and strength, freedom, fulfillment, security, confidence and a clear conscience through my heavenly Father. And because my Father loves me, I will love you, too.

As a teenager, I was about as rebellious as they come. When I purposely became pregnant, my earthly father decided that was the final blow to his heart. He then gave me the ultimatum of adoption or marrying the father of my unborn child and never speaking to him again. I chose marriage. It has been almost fifteen years since I last saw him. I reached out to him a couple of years after my daughter was born, but it was to no avail. He was not ready for a relationship then and I can only hope and pray that he will be ready for one in the future.

I have chosen to forgive him for the choice he made. I have chosen to forgive him for starting a new family without me. I have chosen to forgive him for not wanting to be a part of my life or my children's lives. I have chosen to forgive because God forgave me. I have chosen to see my father through the Lord's eyes. I see a prideful man who is hurting, a gentle man who needs love and a sinful man who needs to be forgiven.

Please understand that I also need to be forgiven. I need him to forgive me. However, the only power I have is through Christ and God's will for our restoration.

The Lord may someday restore our relationship. But until He does, I will continue to pray for my earthly father to forgive me and see me through His heavenly Father's eyes.

The Secret asks us to stop looking at the negative things in our relationships and write down the strengths.

Writing down strengths is certainly an excellent idea. Focus on the positive, yes. Nevertheless, the Truth is we are in a commitment to God first and then to our relationships (2 Corinthians 8:5). God tells us that we can "develop a healthy, robust community that lives right with God and enjoy its results only if you do the hard work of getting along with each other, treating each other with dignity and honor."

We know that in any relationship, whether parent-child, best friends, or husband-wife, there will be difficulty. We become comfortable with each other and consequently we tend to say hurtful things we don't mean or simply get on each other's nerves. It is hard work to treat each other with dignity and honor, especially when we do things that contradict being treated that way. We can become so caught up in the way our loved one is misbehaving that we forget to look within their heart at whose they really are, God's children.

Ephesians 4:2 reminds us to love each other at all times, not just when we see them as lovable. We are asked to not give up on one another, but encourage each other (Hebrews 10:25). Through Christ, we are required to use our God-given gifts to help one another (1 Corinthians 12:7).

Rhonda Byrne takes notice of the fact that we tend to act out how we feel and if we are emitting feelings of respect and love, then we are more likely to receive respect and love from others. Basically, if we love others, they will love back and conversely, if we are hurtful to others, they will be hurtful towards you.

Rick Warren brings an appealing insight: "Respect begins with a godly perspective." One day, the believers in Christ will be heirs of God (Romans 8:17). We should be treating each other with respect and love. For those who don't yet know the Lord, we as Christians need to set the example.

It is impossible to learn to love people who act unlovable without the love of Christ dwelling within us. Even then I have trouble; I have to submit myself to my heavenly Father. There are many mornings when I wake up with a flood of negative thoughts about the people in my life. I can choose to take them with me as I step out of the bed and into my day, or I can offer them up to the Lord and ask Him to give me His perspective of those people. Only then am I able to see that person through God's eyes. Only then am I empowered to think positive thoughts about those whom I feel are unlovable.

My younger sister recently got married. She had a beautiful, magical wedding filled with friends and family. I had the honor of being one of her bridesmaids. Just before the wedding, I began to feel anxiety over the issues with my mother and how this wedding day was going to play out. Would I allow those feelings to get in the way of my sister's special day or would my mother do and say things that may hurt my feelings?

I began to pray that I would be able to focus on God and His plans for my sister and her new husband. I prayed that my mother would do the same and that our day together would be about my sister and not about our family issues.

God answered my prayer. I had to choose to focus on my sister and her delightfully, enchanted day. I chose to love my mom although I didn't feel loved by her. I spoke words of kindness and told her that I loved her. In answered prayer, the entire day was glorious through the grace of God.

I know that He will continue to work through our relationship. I know I can do nothing in my own power to change things, but through the power of Christ's love, our family will one day be restored to the beautiful relationship God intended us to have.

Rick Warren explains this subject in a way that is easily understood. I have included an excerpt from his latest book, *Better Together*:

"Part of listening means we don't rush to fix things or to give an answer; we respect others enough to let them share their full story. Sometimes all we need is for someone to hear what's on our hearts. Respect means we trust others, instead of assuming they will do it wrong, or not do it as well as we would (Philippians 2:3). We also demonstrate respect by the way we talk about others when they aren't around. Nothing destroys relationships faster than gossip (Proverbs 16:28). Respect means, instead of listening to or spreading rumors, we do everything we can to protect the reputation and dignity of our brothers and sisters in Christ. The Bible teaches, 'love covers a multitude of sins' (1 Peter 4:8).

"We excel in showing respect when we work hard at being: Tactful, not just truthful. Tactfulness is thinking before you speak, knowing the way you say something will influence how it is received. Criticism is best received when it is presented in a loving manner, and as mature Christians, we're to "know the whole truth" but "tell it in love" (Ephesians 4:15, MSG). Before you speak frankly with someone, ask yourself, "Why am I saying this? Will my words build them up or tear them down?" 'Kind words bring life but cruel words crush your spirit' (Proverbs 15:4, TEV).

"Understanding, not demanding. We respect others when we treat them the way we would want to be treated (Luke 6:31). When people are dealing with you, do you want them to demand or understand? We should be considerate of one another's feelings and stresses sometimes people don't feel good, and they are having a bad day. The Bible says, 'A wise mature person is known for his understanding' (Proverbs 16:21, TEV).

"Gentle, not judgmental. Even when we disagree with one another, we should still be courteous and respectful – focusing on our own behavior first: '... each of us will give an account of himself to God.

Therefore let us stop passing judgment on each other. Instead, make up your mind not to put any stumbling block in your brother's way' (Romans 14:12-13).

"Polite, not rude. When others are rude to you, you don't have to respond with rudeness. As Christ-followers, we are taught to respond with kindness: 'Don't let evil get the best of you; get the best of evil by doing good' (Romans 12:21, MSG).

"One final note on respect: God entrusted the pastors and spiritual leaders of your church to 'watch over your souls,' and they are accountable to God for this task (Hebrews 13:17, LB). They must correctly teach God's Word; confront false teaching before it spreads; proclaim the gospel to nonbelievers; pray for all people, including you and your family; train and appoint leaders; and they must do this all while serving as an example of what it means to be a follower of Jesus (1 and 2 Timothy; Titus).

"Being tactful, understanding, gentle, and polite doesn't come easy for most of us. But it is all very necessary…Ask God for the strength of the Holy Spirit to enable you to 'excel in showing respect for each other' (Romans 12:10b,GW)."

In Ephesians 5:21, we are told to submit ourselves to one another out of reverence for Christ. Christ submitted Himself to God in everyway, even till death. He did so to save us from Satan, from our eternal death, which gave Christ the authority over those who believe in Him. The authority is that of love and to supply for us every good thing. If we are to live like Christ, we ought to learn to submit ourselves to each other as well.

Relationally, Scripture directs husbands to love their wives just as Christ loves His people. The wife is then commanded by God to submit to her husband. This is not to imply that God is chauvinistic, but to say that because the husband is to love and protect his wife in the same way Christ loves us, wives must yield to their husbands' requests in reverence and honor.

This is something I have struggled with for some time. The order of priority in our lives should be to serve God first, then our spouse. God calls Believers to this standard. For example, if my husband has a list of chores for me to help him with, it is my duty to help him with those chores. But if my husband asks me to lie for him to get him out of a situation, my duty is first to God because He commands me not to lie. God will honor my obedience and therefore correct my husband. Ladies, I can say that this does initially cause friction in the household, but if your husband is the spiritual leader in your home, he will eventually understand and God will bless your obedience.

The Bible tells husbands to love your wives and for wives to respect your husbands (Ephesians 5:23,25). It instructs the children to honor their mother and father (Ephesians 6:2). We are to lead by example to help the poor and needy (Acts 9:36). All of these actions are stemmed from love. If we have not love, we will never see eternal life.

Scripture tells us that love is the greatest commandment. "Love your Lord with all your heart, all your soul and all your mind... Love you neighbor as yourself" (Matthew 22:37-39).

We are called to love one another because Christ loves us.

1 John 3:16, John writes, "...we ought to lay down our lives for our brothers." He says that we must love with actions and in Truth, not just with words. Paul says that, love is patient, kind, and keeps no records of wrongdoing. Love always protects, trusts, hopes and perseveres. But what love doesn't do is envy or boast and it isn't proud. It isn't rude, self-seeking, easily angered or delighting in evil. Love never fails (1 Corinthians 13:4-8).

For those of you who struggle with the idea of perfectionism, know that we are called to be holy because God is holy. That simply means to carry ourselves in high regard because God has commanded us to. We should be people of honor and integrity, people of good character so that we will be held blameless when it comes to how others judge us in our faith.

How we become holy is through direct reliance with God through Christ Jesus. I know from experience this is not an easy way to live. The Lord knows my heart. He knows that it takes His divine Holy Spirit to guide me; for without it, every selfish desire would take over and damage the hearts of those who love me most. I choose love; I pray that you will choose it too.

The Bible says that when you search for God, He will reveal Himself to you. I have known this since I was a child. During my adolescent and young adult years, I prayed. I asked Him to keep me safe and alive. I asked Him to lead me to people who wouldn't hurt me and I promised to do my best to honor Him for the rest of my days.

At that time, I didn't know how to pray in the way I have written in this book. I didn't stop cursing, nor did I stop sinning in any way. But I leaned on God because my faith was all I had left. I knew He heard me because He answered my prayers along the way. He did keep me safe; He did lead me to good, helpful people. He did give me the discernment to know who or what was good for me, but in those gifts, as a part of His gift of free will, He still allowed me to make my own decisions.

Today, I am living my promise to Him. I write to you, passionately, with deep sincerity because I know that if the God in heaven can care for me through all of my sinfulness and love me although I caused so many of His people great pain, that He loves you too.

THE TRUTH ABOUT HEALTH

You may have already realized that *The Secret*'s philosophy to good health is to think good thoughts and you will heal your body. The writers say that when you think negative thoughts, the Universe is blocking positive energy from your cells.

Dr. John Hagelin is a Quantum Physicist who said, "Our body is really the product of our thoughts."

Dr. John Demartini explained the healing art of the placebo effect. He said, "A placebo is something that supposedly has no impact and no effect on the body, like a sugar pill...they have found out that the human mind is the biggest factor in the healing arts, sometimes more so than the medication."

Rhonda Byrne agrees and if people will "think and truly believe ...they will receive what they believe, and they will be cured." She agrees with Dr. Demartini, "healing through the mind can work harmoniously with medicine."

Dr. Ben Johnson, a physician and leader in energy healing said that stress is the cause of disease and different diagnoses. He acknowledges that we all have a built-in immune system that will heal itself.

Dr. Demartini said, "Our physiology creates disease to give us feedback, to let us know we have an unbalanced perspective, or we're not being loving and grateful. So the body's signs and symptoms are not something terrible."

Dr. Johnson says that if we remove physiological stress from the body, it will heal itself.

Collectively, the writers agree that if we think good thoughts, we will be good, healthy people. Morris Goodman summed it up in six words: "Man becomes what he thinks about."

The responsibility of man is to rely upon our Creator to heal us. While there may be a "placebo effect" for many people, the Truth is, the Lord is the One who heals. We have learned that God is in control of every situation and "everything" also applies to our health.

The writers of *The Secret* claim, "Disease is in the body by thought." But what they are omitting is that the "negative thoughts" to which they are referring are a consequence of our sinful nature. We are told by the Apostle Paul to think on all that is good, praiseworthy and lovely. When we don't do that, we are failing to live up to God's desire for us.

The Secret is asking you to look within yourself to call out the goodness and healing from the Universe, while conversely, the Lord asks you to look to Him for Truth and healing.

When I was twenty-one, I went to the gynecologist for an annual checkup. The doctor said everything looked fine and she would call me if there were any problems with the routine tests. Less than a week later, I received a phone call from her. She told me there was a concern and I needed to come back in so that she could explain the results of the Pap smear with me.

While in the office for the second time that week, she told me I had cancerous cells on my cervix and they needed to be frozen off in order to prevent them from multiplying into full blown cancer. She said it was a simple outpatient procedure and I needed to schedule it as soon as possible. I didn't have any insurance at the time and I was extremely nervous about having the procedure.

I prayed for God to heal me. Even in my most immature, naïve mind, I knew that if God wanted me free of cancer, He would have to do it. Through prayer, I realized I would have to have the procedure.

A short time later, I encouraged my boyfriend to go to church with me. I confessed the outcome of the doctor's visit to my boyfriend, I repented of every awful thing I had done, and changed my way of life to honor the Lord. I started reading the Bible and searching for answers within our friends at church. My thirst for knowledge was insatiable and God led me to the answers.

I continued to live with my boyfriend, which I knew wasn't what God would have chosen. I rationalized that after five years of living together and moving with my daughter over a thousand miles with him, we couldn't possibly live separately. Nick and

I talked about getting married and after five years of dating, he proposed.

A couple of years had gone by since the procedure. When I became pregnant with my second child, I decided to go to a free clinic to determine the validity of my at home pregnancy test. They confirmed the pregnancy and sent me to have another gynecological visit.

Sitting in the waiting area, I thought about my last visit with the doctor. I prayed that the procedure had destroyed my cancerous cells and that none had come back. Once again, the doctor said, everything looked fine and they would call me in a couple of days if anything were "abnormal." In the meantime, I was to schedule my next prenatal visit.

Weeks went by without a phone call. I wondered if they had missed something, or if the procedure had worked. At the next prenatal visit, I told them about my last experience with the doctor. They examined the information and concluded that I must have been healed.

Thank you, God in Heaven who heals.

God told Moses, "I am the Lord, the one who heals you" (Exodus 15:26, GNB). God instructs us to seek his will and guidance for our lives. He promises to heal us if we would turn to Him. He said, [If] "my people who are called by my name humble themselves and pray, and seek my face and turn from their wicked ways, then I will hear from heaven, will forgive their sin, and will heal their land" (2 Chronicles 7:14, NASB).

The writers of *The Secret* said that is was better to get on with your life than to worry about your ailments. Many people do walk around telling everyone of their problems and pains, which could lead to more sickness. But I urge you to listen to what God says.

In Jeremiah 30: 15-17, God said, "Why do you cry out over your injury? Your pain is incurable. Because your iniquity is great and your sins are numerous, I have done these things to you...for I will restore you to health and I will heal you of your wounds...(NASB)

Are you in need of a healer? Physically? Mentally? Spiritually? Gilead cried out to God, "Heal me, O Lord, and I will be healed, save me and I will be saved, for Thou art my praise" Jeremiah 17:14, NASB). You too can cry out to the Lord to be saved from any infirmity brought upon you, physically, mentally and spiritually. It is important to first understand that in order to obtain complete restoration of health, healing and obedience are essential. Remember God said, "I am the Lord, the One who heals you."

The American Standard Bible explains this well in Exodus 15:26, "And He said, 'If you give earnest heed to the voice of Lord your God, and do what is right in His sight, and give ear to His commandments, and keep all His statutes, I will put none of the diseases on you which I have put on the Egyptians; for I, the Lord, am your healer.'"

I am a living example of giving earnest heed to the voice of my Lord, my God. I turned from my old way of living and did what God wanted me to do. It wasn't easy, actually, it is one of the most difficult things I have had to do, but God walked with me through it all. Now, not only have those cancerous cells disintegrated, but I also have a special place in the kingdom of God.

Rhonda Byrne said, "All stress begins with one negative thought…No matter what you might have manifested, you can change it…with one small positive thought and then another."

The Truth is we can change it, but not by our own power. The positive thought must be in Christ. As a result of our own sinful nature, and placing the faith within the universal spiritual forces, and ourselves, God has asked us to open our eyes so that we may see the Truth. The Truth is Jesus is all we need. The Bible says to the Believer, "You died with Christ, now the forces of the Universe don't have any power over you…so why bother with the rules that humans have made up. Obeying these rules may seem to be the smart thing to do. They appear to make you love God more and to be very humble and to have control over your body. But they don't really have any power over our desires" (Colossians 2:20,21-23 CEV).

When we submit to the Lord and are obedient to Him, he is faithful and will heal our diseases (2 Kings 20:1-5).

Our God is loving and just. He will do what it takes to bring you to Him and if you choose otherwise, He says that you will undergo suffering, (you will be disciplined). This isn't because He is despicable and vile; it is because He loves you; it is for your benefit, so that you will turn from your ways and love Him. "And the Lord will strike...striking but healing; so they will return to the Lord, and He will respond to them and heal them" (Isaiah 19:22, NASB).

I believe that my "abnormal" results of the Pap smear were God's way of telling me that it's time for me to fulfill my promise to Him. He allowed me to undergo suffering so that I would turn to Him for help. He does love me. He struck me, but healed me so that I would return to Him.

Remember, God knew from the beginning that you would sin and that many would reject Him. God sent His Son for you. "...But He was pierced for our transgressions, He was crushed for our iniquities; the chastening for our well-being fell upon Him, and by His scourging we are healed" (Isaiah 53:5, NASB).

The Psalmist, knowing the sovereignty of God, thanked Him for his affliction. "Before I was afflicted I went astray, but now I obey your word...It was good for me to be afflicted so that I might learn your decrees...I know, O LORD, that your laws are righteous, and in faithfulness you have afflicted me" (Psalm 119:67,71,75).

I am not saying that all sin leads to poor health, but you must confront the sin. God says, "He who conceals his transgressions will not prosper, but he who confesses and renounces them will find mercy."

God's mercy for me was not only to bring me to His feet, but He also gave me the family I always longed for.

"Blessed is the man who always fears the Lord, but he who hardens his heart falls into trouble" (Proverbs 28:14). The most important issue here is when you are hurting in any way, I urge you to ask for healing from your Father in heaven who wants so desperately to have your attention and love.

Once you have sought the Father's will, look for a possible root of the pain. David wrote, "I am full of anxiety because of my sin" (Psalm 38:18, NASB). Pray, "Search me, O God, and know my heart; test me and know my anxious thoughts; and see if there is any offensive way in me, and lead me in the way everlasting."

God will always honor our obedience; He has the power and authority to pardon all your iniquities and heal all your diseases.

Rhonda Byrne refers to "three magnificent powers of operation – the power of gratitude to heal, the power of faith to receive, and the power of laughter and joy to dissolve disease in our bodies."

Dr. Ben Johnson reminds us that our bodies have the innate ability to heal themselves by removing physiological stress from them.

While I may have removed the physiological stress from my mind, I also gave it to God. He took my stress and gave me the peace that can only be found through knowing His Son, Jesus Christ.

I suppose you can try to heal yourself by your own power, but the Apostle Paul tells us in 1 Corinthians 1:25, "For the foolishness of God is wiser than man's wisdom, and the weakness of God is stronger than man's strength."

The Lord will heal you, but it is important to remember His grace is sufficient for you. The Lord may have healed me physically, but the effects of my sinful nature and wrong choices during my young adult life still remain. I can't change the damage I have caused myself emotionally or mentally; I must rely on the Lord for that.

Sometimes, God will allow the infirmity to remain while healing you emotionally, just like the apostle Paul. We know from 2 Corinthians 12:7 that Paul pleaded with the Lord to take away the "thorn in his flesh" (something wrong with his body) and Jesus' response was, "My grace is sufficient for you, for my power is made perfect in weakness." Jesus had a better solution than to remove Paul's "thorn." Jesus wants our human weakness to provide the ideal opportunity for the display of His divine power.

Proverbs 14:30 says, "Peace of mind makes the body healthy..." (GNB) Paul made it his priority to have a peaceful attitude about his weakness so that others would be able to see his peace and know that it must only come from God. On the other hand, if Paul had dwelled on his imperfection, he would have taken away from the work of the Lord.

The Lord says to focus on Him, on His will for you and everything else will be given to you. Give thanks to the Lord for His mercy and power to heal you, receive the free gift He has given and He will give you joy. The Lord God created you and your body. If the body has the inherit ability to heal itself, can't we then agree that the Lord is the One who heals?

The Secret says, "Beliefs about aging are all in our minds...focus on eternal youth."

King David knew the truth; he praised our Father for forgiving our sins, healing our disease, redeeming our life from the pit, and renewing our youth (Psalm 103:3-5). David knew that only God's healing would renew his spirit and make him feel like a youth again. Don't worry about getting older.

Proverbs 16:31 says, "Long life is a reward of the righteous, gray hair is a glorious crown." "The glory of young men is their strength, gray hair the splendor of the old" (Proverbs 20:29). But youth and age are meaningless if one doesn't know the Lord. Focus not on eternal youth, but on eternal life.

The Truth to health is to seek God. Thank Him for the health you have and ask Him what His will for you is. Ask him what sin He sees in your heart and repent from those sins. Ask God how you can honor and obey Him. Be still and listen for His reply. Ask Him to heal you and if He physically doesn't heal, take comfort knowing that because of your repentance and obedience to Him, your soul will be saved and your spirit will live with Him for all eternity. Praise your heavenly Father for that!

THE TRUTH ABOUT THE WORLD

"Peace can't be achieved through violence only through understanding." Albert Einstein

The Secret claims that we can achieve peace through a process of thinking good thoughts. Jesus said, "I have told you this, so that you might have peace in your hearts because of me. While you are in the world, you will have to suffer. But cheer up! I have defeated the world" (John 16:33, CEV).

While this world will never be peaceful and free of war, (world wars or civil wars) I believe it is possible for us to achieve peace in our hearts, if we would combine these processes. Scriptures say that God gives peace beyond understanding to those who are in Christ Jesus (Philippians 4:7).

The key to peace is to know Jesus Christ. Therefore, "Set your mind on things above [heavenly, eternal things], not on things on the earth" (Colossians 3:2).

The Secret invites you to look at this world through a positive perspective, to turn your mind away from negative thinking and start looking at what we can do and can achieve. Byrne referred to teacher and author, Hale Dwoskin, who said, "What we focus on we do create, for instance, at a war that's going on, or strife, or suffering, we're adding our energy to it. We're pushing ourselves, and that only creates resistance." In essence what she is saying is what we resist will continue to persist.

The Secret teaches us to focus on trust, love, abundance, education, and peace. The writers say, "To change anything, go within and emit a new signal with your thoughts and feelings."

The Truth is, feelings do come from thoughts, and while we can't always control our feelings, we can control how we think. This is the will of God.

Philippians 4:8, "...Brothers, whatever is true, whatever is noble, whatever is right, whatever is pure, whatever is lovely, whatever is admirable, if anything is excellent or praiseworthy, think about such things. Whatever you have learned or received from me put it into practice. And the God of peace will be with you."

The Scripture is saying that when you meditate on God's word and remain in prayer, He will free your worries and anxieties. You can't control the world, but with the Lord's help, you can have peace and freedom that comes from within.

"Everything in this world began with one thought. Then those thoughts and emotions keep that very event in our existence and make it bigger. If we took our minds off it and focused instead on love, it could not exist..." Rhonda Byrne, *The Secret*.

Couldn't we say that if we first focus on what was True, we would know exactly where to place our attention? God said to place our hearts in His hand; to seek first the kingdom of God and the rest will be given. That's Truth.

We can certainly focus our attention on love. That would fulfill the obedience to what Paul said in Philippians 4:8. But we must go beyond love. When it comes to determining the Truth of God, of His Word, versus what the world says, we are called to bring our attention to not only what is true, but we must also make it a practice to do the things which are worthy of praise, noble, righteous, and pure. Those are the actions we must take to make this world a better place.

However, the reality is that not everyone will want to do what is right and if they want to, they may choose not to – hence the way of the world today. So what are we going to do about it? Simply thinking "world peace" will not do the job. Not everyone will partake in the act of achieving world peace, so what then are we to do? We are called to pray.

Only God in heaven will help the world. We are required to put our faith in Him, that is our responsibility. God's responsibility is to respond to us. Faith is an action word, it means not only to pray to Him for help and deliverance from war and conflict, but we are to act according to the direction He gives.

As prince of this world, Satan has a devised plan for the nations. His desire is to defuse God's plan by means of war and destruction. For that reason, Satan will fool you into thinking that your efforts alone are satisfying the world's desire for peace. But be on your guard, as soon as you think all is good, the devil is quick to deceive you.

That is why we must have Jesus, why we must know the Truth of God, so that we can withstand the snares of the devil.

The Truth of the world is that it will end (Matthew 24:6). The Truth is, as believers in Christ, we all have a responsibility to help one another while we are here in this world (Hebrews 13:1). What kind of legacy do you want to leave your children and your children's children? Is it one of monetary value that can only be spent and used up? Or have you thought about providing the gift of eternal life, the True peace of Jesus Christ?

Jesus said to his disciples, "I do not give to you as the world gives. Do not let your hearts be troubled and do not be afraid" (John 14:37).

> "I believe the Bible is the best gift God has ever given to man. All the good from the Savior of the world is communicated to us through this book." Abraham Lincoln

> "It is impossible to rightly govern the world without God and the Bible." George Washington

THE TRUTH ABOUT YOU

The Secret teaches you to think positively about yourself, to use words of affirmation instead of doubt. Rhonda Byrne wants you to start saying, "I am" and say something positive after that beginning. She says it's a "shortcut" to receiving what you are and what you want. She said, "Well, now you know you are the Supreme Mind and that you can draw anything you want from that One Supreme Mind." She refers to the "One Supreme Mind" as the invisible field that supplies you with what you desire. It could be anything whether you call it the "Universe, the Supreme Mind, God, Infinite Intelligence, or whatever else." She claims that is "the law."

I hope we have established that there is only one God, known as the Father, the Creator, the Son, the Holy Spirit, the Giver, and the Healer. God is the Supreme Mind and the Infinite Intelligence. His law is to seek Him first, with love.

Scripture warns us, "Human wisdom, brilliance and insight – they are of no help if the Lord is against you" (Proverbs 21:30).

BE AWARE OF YOUR THOUGHTS

Rhonda Byrne was right when she told us to be aware of our thoughts. She said they could get away from us if we let them, but "when you are aware... you know what you are thinking. You have gained control of your thoughts, and that is where all your power is."

Remember, we don't have the power ourselves. The power comes from Christ who is in the Believer. Therefore, we must take every thought captive to the obedience of Christ because we are who *He* says we are. Our thoughts come from our hearts and if we have the Lord within, we will believe what He says we are. "So as he thinketh in his heart, so is he" (Proverbs 23:7, KJV).

Byrne reminds us that we must "remember to remember" to ask the Universe to remind you who you are. However, the difference is, she asks the Universe to give her a nudge to bring back to the present whenever her mind has taken over and is having a party at her expense. But we (Christians) are called to ask the Lord, our Father to help us remember what is true of us.

Remember, the mind can be the devil's playground. Satan wants us to think poorly of ourselves; he wants us to be miserable Christians so that we would deny the Truth and rebel against God. As a result, he puts thoughts into our head that are untrue.

When "we demolish all arguments and every pretension that sets itself up against the knowledge of God, and we take captive every thought to make it obedient to Christ" (2 Corinthians 10:5) then we will have defeated the enemy and what we know from God will exist to be true! Amen. After that defeat and realization, we can do anything in Christ.

Thus, the real secret of power is consciousness of the power of Christ. As you study the Truths that God has given, you will then be able to live freely from the chains of mental warfare.

ARE YOU NOT YOUR PAST?

Rhonda Byrne writes, "You are not your past." She claims that if we focus on the hardships of the past, we will bring them into the present and thus create the same difficulties in the future. She encourages us to let the past go and "unleash the magic" that comes with focusing on the life you deserve.

Byrne is right when she said we should not focus on the stuff in the past, but we do need to acknowledge it. We need to know that if we don't seek the wisdom of the Lord, we will never be able to change our mistakes. The difference between changing ourselves and allowing the Lord to change us is that "the foolishness of God is wiser than the wisdom of man" (1 Corinthians 1:25). We are fools to think that we can call on the Universe to change us and still believe that will give us freedom in life.

Michael Bernard Beckwith said we could break ourselves free from our "heredity patterns, cultural codes, and social beliefs" if we focus on the power within us that is greater than the power within the world.

The Truth is we are all cursed with generational sin. It has been present since the sin of Adam and Eve. We are therefore, cursed with a sinful nature.

We discussed earlier that Satan is the power in this world and unless we give our life to Jesus and let Him be the Lord over our lives, we will succumb to the ways of the devil. The only way we can defeat the power within the world is through acceptance of and obedience to Jesus Christ.

Byrne said, "It is a good idea to become aware when you say, 'I'm not' and think about what you are creating as you say it." She said it is a good idea to use the words "I AM" when you are describing yourself. She wants you to believe you are "whole, perfect, strong, powerful, loving, harmonious, and happy."

Of course we want to believe that we are perfect, whole, strong, harmonious and happy people. But we are not all of those things. Most of us in our human nature are not perfect or harmonious or happy. Most of us find faults with ourselves from head to toe, inside and out. Is there a way to believe you are a strong person, emotionally or mentally? Is there a way to believe you are absolutely perfect? On your own there is no way you can say that without lying to yourself.

The Truth is that we must rely on the Lord to help us become that way. He says that through our faith in Jesus Christ, we are made righteous and the effect of righteousness is peace, which is harmony. Unless you are fooling yourself, the only way to honestly believe we are all of those things is to believe God when He tells you that you are made perfect through your faith in Jesus Christ. God gives you peace when you accept His Son as your personal Savior.

This is the phenomenal beauty of our faith in Christ. We don't have to be perfect or feel badly because alone we aren't strong and perfect. It is Jesus Christ who is all those things in us. God says we are His children when we acknowledge His Son as the one who died for our eternal life. As God's children, through His eyes, we are joint heirs with Christ in His kingdom; we are perfect, we are strong, we are harmonious, we are happy, and we are loved.

As God's children, we are to ask Him to empower us. If we tell ourselves that we are powerful and strong and perfect and loving without asking the Lord to empower us, we are only fooling ourselves and living a counterfeit Christian life. Instead of lying to ourselves, we can ask our heavenly Father to replace our lies with Truth, with the Holy Spirit.

The Holy Spirit is the one that will guide you in your life with Christ. The Holy Spirit will help you become obedient to God. Life with the Spirit will give you love, joy, peace, endurance, kindness, goodness, faithfulness, gentleness, the self-control to be truthful when you say, "I am..." You won't have to convince yourself that you are something you aspire to be because through Christ and the help of the Holy Spirit, you already are! Praise God!

The Secret and other self-help books of the like are fooling you into believing you are your own god. The Truth is we yearn for someone to see us in the way we aspire to be. We are "attention-seekers" and "do-gooders." We want people to praise us for the wonderful people we are and aspire to become. God put that desire in you, but He wants the glory for it. Please don't be fooled by *The Secret*. Place your faith in Jesus Christ, not a book that can be destroyed, not some earthly, "universal" principles that will fade away when you do.

Gregory Dickow is the Founder and Pastor of Life Changers International Church in Hoffman Estates, Illinois. His ministry reaches thousands of people searching for the Truth. He believes that a successful life comes from living obediently for the Lord. He believes that when you walk with the Holy Spirit as your guide, you can achieve the dreams that Christ has set for you. His ministry comes from Isaiah 32:17,20: "The fruit of righteousness will be peace; the effect of righteousness will be quietness and confidence forever. How blessed you will be..."

The law of the Lord is perfect, reviving the soul (Psalm 19:7). From the heart of the human spirit come emotions, thoughts, motivations, courage and actions. Proverbs 10:24 states, "The righteous get what they want, but the wicked will get what they fear most" (GNB).

Pastor Dickow has a personal confession chart that he often recites. If you want to have the life you have dreamed, this may be the tool to get you there. Again, *The Secret* has some validity; it just lacks the wisdom and presence of the Lord. The only "Law" is the law of God. Remember, we have established that once we make a decision to follow Jesus, He is the mediator between God and us. Therefore, anything we ask in the name of Jesus, He will give – if we are living with the Holy Spirit, in His will. God's will is for us to love Him, pray to Him, and serve Him. God loves us and He wants to bless us. With that forefront knowledge, and unwavering faith, God will answer our prayers.

Say these out loud daily. Believe they will happen and trust God to let it. These are the words from Pastor Dickow's Personal Confession:

> "I set the course of my life today with my words: I declare today that I will not be defeated, discouraged, depressed or disappointed today. I am the head, I have insight, I have wisdom, I have ideas, and I have authority. I exercise my authority today with my words and I decree a thing and it is so. Greater is He that is in me than he that is in the world (1 John 4:4)…the same Spirit that raised Jesus from the dead, lives in me…(Romans 8:11). As I speak words today, they come to pass (Job 22:28); they go before me, they bring the things to pass that I desire; and they stop all attacks, assaults, oppression, and fear from coming to my life. God is on my side today and therefore I cannot be defeated. His favor surrounds me today as a shield. (Psalm 5:12) I expect favor today from heaven and earth. Jesus had favor with God and man (Luke 2:52), and as he is, so am I on this earth. (1 John 4:17) Therefore, I have favor today with God and man. I expect and

receive favor in my home, favor in my job, favor in my business, favor in my ministry, favor with my finances, and favor in every deal I am involved in... I have the wisdom of God today. I will think the right thoughts, say the right words and make the right decisions in every situation I face today. My mouth speaks wisdom and my heart is filled with understanding. (Psalm 49:3) I ask for, and receive, an abundant supply of wisdom and understanding today from God (James 1:5)... wisdom from above, and wisdom that is pure, peaceable, gentle, unwavering, willing to yield, without hypocrisy. (James 3:17) Wisdom and understanding are better than silver and gold and nothing I desire can compare with them; therefore, I make it my ambition and desire to have understanding and wisdom; therefore I know I will have all of the other desires of my heart (Proverbs 8:10-11). My words go before me in securing my divine health and healing... I will not be sick today; I will not be sad today; I will not be broke today; I will not be confused today. I will have health today, I will have joy today; I will have all the money I need in the name of Jesus. My steps are ordered by the Lord... (Psalm 37:23) I have a covenant with God and by the blood of Jesus I release my divine protection and divine provision. My angels are carrying out the Word of God on my behalf...I receive supernatural strength and encouragement from God and my angels. Angels carry out the Word of God and every word that I speak that lines up with the Word of God is being carried out by angels, even now as I speak (Psalm 103:20). I expect to have divine appointments today, to run into the right people, and to be delivered from the wrong people. Any adversity, attack, accidents and tragedies that were headed my way are diverted right now in Jesus' name. I speak to the raging waters in my life: peace, be still. I say to my emotions, peace, be still. I say to my mind, peace, be still. I say to my body, peace, be still. I say to my home, peace, be still. I say to my family, peace, be still. Now I speak to: every mountain of fear, every mountain of discouragement, every mountain of stress, every mountain of depression, every mountain of lack and insufficiency And I say, 'Be removed and cast into the sea in Jesus name!' (Mark 11:23) I expect the best day of my life spiritually, emotionally, relationally and financially today in Jesus name!"

Wow, Amen! If that doesn't get your body and mind energized for the Lord, you, my friend must not have a pulse.

Charles Haanel, author of *The Master Key System* said, "The real secret of power is consciousness of power."

The Truth is the Holy Spirit is the real power. As you become aware of the power that the Holy Spirit has in you, the Believer, you will begin to use it to serve your heavenly Father. That Spirit will fill you with the love of Jesus and you will know the power and strength of the Lord. As the Holy Spirit fills you with understanding, you will begin to receive the answers to all your questions from Him. If you are seeking guidance in your life, ask the Lord to show you and through the Holy Spirit, it will be revealed to you.

Rhonda Byrne said, "The truth is that the Universe has been answering you all of your life, but you cannot receive the answers unless you are aware. Be aware of everything around you, because you are receiving the answers to your questions in every moment of the day."

The Truth is the Lord has been tugging at your heart. He has been persuing you all of your life. If you have a yearning for answers to your life and who you are, the Lord, your Father created you, ask Him for the answers. He will give you all you have ever needed and more.

Yes, be aware of everything around you; you may be receiving some answers to your questions, but are those from the Holy Spirit, or the devil? Take the thought, the answer to God's Word, the Bible, to see if what you are receiving is from God or Satan.

Byrne explains that everything we want is motivated by love. We must focus on ourselves fully and focus on the presence within you. She asks us to sit still and feel the presence within.

If I focus on what is within me, isn't that selfishness, which is not rooted in love? Be careful! We have learned that God asks us to "Be still and know I am God." If I focus on myself and not God, my love comes from self-centeredness. The Truth is that real, authentic love comes from God. All of your imperfections will be changed as a result of your obedience to Christ, who exemplifies the true meaning of love.

THE TRUTH ABOUT LIFE

Neale Donald Walsch is an author, international speaker and a spiritual messenger. He says, "There is no blackboard in the sky on which God has written your purpose. Your purpose is what you say it is. Your mission is the mission you give yourself and no one will stand in judgment of it now or ever."

While there may not be a "blackboard" in the sky, there is a clear mission for each one of us – it's found in the Bible. King David wrote in Psalm 139:16, "You saw me before I was born. The days allotted for me have been recorded in your book before any of them ever began" (GNB). God has a clear mission and plan for your life.

Scripture says when you search for God you will find Him. He has revealed Himself to all so that people are without excuse (Romans 1:20). Jesus clearly stated that our mission is to love God with all our heart, soul, mind and strength. Second, our mission is to love each other (Mark 12:30,31). When we have love, true agape love, then we will know the fullness of God.

Jesus said, "...I have come so that they may have life and have it to the full" (John 10:10). Jesus is the Way, the Truth, and the Life. No one comes to God or Heaven except through belief in Jesus Christ.

If you believe with all your heart and confess with your mouth that Jesus Christ is Lord, that God raised Him from the dead then you shall be saved (Romans 10:9). It is that simple. Once we acknowledge that Truth and accept Him as our Heavenly Father, we will able to learn how to love Him. He will teach us, mold us and show us our personal "blackboard."

Jack Canfield, author and contributor to *The Secret*, said he thought for many years that "there was something I was supposed to do, and if I wasn't doing it, God wouldn't be happy with me. When I really understood that my primary aim was to feel and experience joy, then I began to do only those things which brought me joy."

An awesome revelation of God is that He already knows what you are or are not going to do – He has seen the beginning of time and the end of time on earth. You cannot disappoint God because He already knows what you will do.

The key to finding your purpose in life is to put the Lord first in all you do, whether or not it makes you happy. Sometimes we start out doing a task that God has asked us to do with the thought of misery and complications attached to the assignment. But once you have finished the task, you end up being blessed by the experience.

I stated earlier, when I first learned of *The Secret*, my first response was to tell everyone what the Truth really is. I had an overwhelming sensation that this would be it! I would finally write my first book and kick off my writing career. I would finally fulfill my promise to God and use the gift of writing as my ministry for Him.

I didn't pray about it, though. A few weeks passed and I soon forgot about *The Secret*. My husband and I have our favorite shows that we record and watch on our "TV nights." We had recorded that particular *Oprah Show* and had not yet deleted it. I played the episode again.

Those same emotions stirred in me, but this time I prayed about it. I asked the Lord if this is His plan for me. But, I had my doubts in my own abilities. I expressed that I wasn't well educated and I am not "qualified" according to the publishing companies. I didn't think I would be able to get the Truth out there.

As I was praying, the Lord reminded me of Moses. He argued with God from the moment God chose him to lead the people out of Egypt. Moses told God that he too was slow in speech and incapable of leading the people. But the Lord used Moses anyway. Not only did Moses lead the people out of Egypt and into God's promised land, but he also had the indescribable experience of talking with God, walking with God and doing God's work.

It was the reminder of Moses that gave me hope. I didn't know where this book would lead, but if God asked me to do it, then He will make this book a success, even if only one person's life was lead to God.

I began to write down all the questionable comments I heard on that show and the next day, my husband brought home the book of *The Secret*. I read it in about a day and began to write.

The first two days were amazing! I prayed as I wrote. I asked the Lord to help me find the appropriate scriptures and He did! I felt closer to Him than I have ever felt. The next few days, however, were completely different. I was confused and concerned because I couldn't see where I was going with it. I doubted whether or not I could write and really, what more could I say that hadn't already been said?

Well, about six months later, this book was written. The Lord guided me each step of the way. The blessings have been innumerable. I have a new respect for the Lord who I now am comfortable calling, "My Father."

All other principles of faith in Christ will come to you as you ask. Jesus was talking to His disciples (the people who believed He was the Son of God) when He told them, "ask anything in my name and it will be given to you"(Matthew 21:22). He also told his disciples that if they had faith as small as a mustard seed, they would be able to move mountains; nothing would be impossible (Matthew 17:20). Faith is the secret to life – faith in Jesus Christ. Faith comes from hearing the message and the message is heard through the Word of Christ (Romans 10:17). Therefore, we must know Christ as God's Son before we are able to move mountains.

It is true that we can have what we want, as long as God allows it. See, when we delight ourselves in

God, He will give us the desires of our hearts (Psalm 37:4). When we are looking for answers from the Lord, he loves us enough to supply us with abundance. We will be doing what gives us joy and pleasure because He knows our innermost thoughts and He searches our hearts (Psalm 7:9).

Dr. John Hagelin, co-author of *The Secret* and quantum physicist, educator, and public policy expert wrote, "Inner happiness actually is the fuel of success."

When we ask the Lord for our purpose in life, He is faithful to give us the desire of our heart. For out of the heart flows the wellspring of life (Proverbs 4:23). Inner happiness only comes from joy in the Lord. And yes, Dr. Hagelin is right; when we receive the joy from the Lord we will have the fuel of success in all things.

Max Lucado recently wrote *Cure For The Common Life: Living in Your Sweet Spot*. He distinctively explains how we can be used for God's purpose. "Each person is given something to do that shows who God is" (1 Corinthians 12:7 MSG). Lucado motivates us "to use your uniqueness make a big deal about God... every day of your life." He illustrates it this way: "Use your uniqueness (what you do) to make a big deal out of God (why you do it) everyday of your life (where you do it)." The center of those three principles, according to Lucado is where you will find your "sweet spot." That is where you will thrive and succeed in everything you do – because you are doing it for God.

Society has lost sight of that fact. We have a propensity to want to use our gifts the Lord has given us to glorify ourselves. Many athletes credit their success to hard work and tenacity, actors tend to flaunt their worldly rewards and use them for more publicity, and everyday people are parading around with expensive cars and designer clothing. The fact is most of them are miserable. Because we were created to glorify God, man has an innate, longing desire to find the meaning of his or her life. Many of us think that we will find fulfillment in our jobs – maybe because it pays well or it "looks good" to society. Many of us think we will find joy in having a family or finding the right person to "complete" us. But the truth is, that belief is deceiving, and consequently we are a lost nation.

Lucado explains that when we look back at our life, we need to look at those times when we thrived. Were you good at cheerleading or debate? Did you like to write or draw? Were you the one people always came to for advice? Look at your strengths and notice how you felt and what those feelings produced. Did they produce happiness and peace? As those feelings unfold, you can begin to apply those strengths to your future.

What is the thing you did well and brought you contentment? God put it there. Before you were born, he crafted you, sculpted you – you are God's masterpiece. He knows every detail in you, on you and about you because He put it there. "God planned and packed you on purpose for His purpose." Accept this truth; remember your childhood, seek the Lord's wisdom and guidance to find His purpose for you. And do it. That is the secret to life.

EMBRACE WHO YOU ARE

Byrne writes, "The earth turns on its orbit for you. The oceans ebb and flow for you. The birds sing for you. The sun rises and it sets for you. The stars come out for you. Every beautiful thing you see, every wondrous thing you experience is all there for you. No matter whom you thought you were, now you know the Truth of you who you really are. You are the heir to the kingdom."

Your Father in heaven created them for you. The universe hasn't created anything. In your Father's hands is where you will find life.

When you apply these Truths to your life, you will soon discover the power that is within you, which comes from the Holy Spirit. That power within you, which comes from the Lord, will give you wisdom, love and joy. Jesus is the answer to all that has been, all that is, and all that will ever be.

From the words of Beth Moore, I invite you to pray this prayer daily in your life. This prayer, with a humble heart will help you with your relationship with the Lord. Pray, believe, act, and receive the gifts Your Father has been longing to give.

"I belong to God. I am a holy vessel because I house the Holy Spirit of the Living God. The Lord of heaven and earth has said over me, 'I declare you holy.' Today I commit to start believing what He says. I am holy. Empower me daily, Spirit of the Living

God, to treat myself as holy. Open my eyes to every scheme of the enemy to treat me as if I'm not. You, God are God. Your Word is Truth. This day, Father, I choose to believe You. In Jesus Name, Amen."

"May the God of hope fill you with all joy and peace as you trust in Him, so that you may overflow with hope by the power of the Holy Spirit" (Romans 15:13).

REFERENCES

According to the Secret:
>*The Oprah Show*, (2007). Episode on April 16, 2007, Harpo Productions
>
>Byrne, Rhonda, (2006). *The Secret*, Simon & Schuster Inc.

The Father of Lies:
>*Bible Questions Answered*, (2002-2008). Retrieved June 8, 2007 from <u>www.gotquestions.org</u>, Got Questions Ministries

The Truth Revealed:
>*Bible Questions Answered*, (2002-2008). Retrieved May 2007 from <u>www.gotquestions.org</u>, Got Questions Ministries

How To Use The Truth:
>White, James Emery, (2005). *The Prayer God Longs For*, InterVarsity Press, p.21,29
>
>Hybels, Bill, (1998). *Too Busy Not To Pray*, InterVarsity Press, p.64

Chambers, Oswald, (1992). *My Utmost For His Highest*, Discovery House Publishers, p. May 18

Crowe, Bruce, (2006, 2007). www.ChristianQuotes.org, Retrieved May 2007

God's Powerful Process:

Chambers, Oswald, (1992). *My Utmost For His Hi3ghest*, Discovery House Publishers, p. February 12

The Truth About Money:

Crowe, Bruce, (2006, 2007). www.ChristianQuotes.org, Retrieved May 2007

The Truth About Relationships:

Warren, Rick. (2004). *Better Together: What on earth are we here for?* Purpose Driving Publishing Ed.2.0, p. 12,13,17

The Truth About The World:

Crowe, Bruce, (2006, 2007). www.ChristianQuotes.org, Retrieved June 2007

The Truth About You:

Dickow, Gregory (2006), *Pastor Dickow's Personal Confession*, Internet Retrieved June 15, 2007 from www.lifechangerschurch.com

Crowe, Bruce, (2006, 2007). www.ChristianQuotes.org, Retrieved June 2007

The Truth About Life:
> Lucado, Max, (2006). *Cure for the Common Life: Living in Your Sweet Spot*, Nelson Publishers, W Publishing Group, p.24
>
> Moore, Beth, (2006). *Daniel*, Closing Benediction, LifeWay Press

Printed in the United States
119853LV00001B/184-1149/P